DIRK BOGARDE

———

GREAT MEADOW

PENGUIN BOOKS

PENGUIN BOOKS

Published by the Penguin Group
Penguin Books Ltd, 27 Wrights Lane, London W8 5TZ, England
Penguin Books USA Inc., 375 Hudson Street, New York, New York 10014, USA
Penguin Books Australia Ltd, Ringwood, Victoria, Australia
Penguin Books Canada Ltd, 10 Alcorn Avenue, Toronto, Ontario, Canada M4V 3B2
Penguin Books (NZ) Ltd, 182–190 Wairau Road, Auckland 10, New Zealand

Penguin Books Ltd, Registered Offices: Harmondsworth, Middlesex, England

First published by Viking 1992
Published in Penguin Books 1993
3 5 7 9 10 8 6 4

Printed in England by Clays Ltd, St Ives plc

This book is for

LALLY

and to the memory of my parents

Author's Note

An evocation, this, of the happiest days of my childhood: 1930–34. The world was gradually falling apart all around me, but I was serenely unaware. I was not, alas, the only ostrich.

I have altered some of the names and amalgamated many of their characteristics, so no single person existed exactly as I have written them to be: they are all part of the evocation. Except, that is, for my own family and that of Lally. The dialogue, of course, is reconstructed to as near the original as I can remember. Events have been slightly rearranged to make the spread of four years containable. But this is how it was sixty years ago. For those who have forgotten, or those who never knew, here is a modest list which might be helpful.

M.Y.O.B.	'Mind Your Own Business.'
Family Hold Back	At table with guests.
O.M.	'Officina Meccanica': A splendid Italian sporting car.
Adolf Hitler	Began causing *serious* disquiet and fear in 1930. In 1934, with a staggering majority vote of 90 per cent, he became the President of Germany. In 1933 the first trickle of Jews started to arrive in England fleeing persecution.

R.101	The greatest airship (British) in the world. Crashed on a French hillside in 1930, on a voyage to India.
Emperor of Abyssinia	Ras Tafari was crowned Emperor in 1930 and became Haile Selassie.
Gunter's	A very famous, and highly fashionable, tea-shop in Mayfair.
Caledonian Market	An enormous flea-market in the East End.
Pip, Squeak and Wilfred	A popular children's comic-strip.
The Long Man (of Wilmington)	One of the world's largest representations of a human figure. Possibly seventh century.
Trolley buses	Appeared on the streets in 1931, and Sunday cinemas were made legal at the same time.
Mrs Lindbergh	Wife of Charles Lindbergh, the first man to fly solo over the Atlantic. Their twenty-month-old baby was kidnapped and murdered in 1932.
The Cunarder	Launched on Clydebank in September 1934, the *Queen Mary* was familiarly known as the *534*.

Fanny Blake, the most valiant of editors, has wrestled hard and long with my *deliberately* limited vocabulary and re-

moved as many *and*s, *so*s and *which*s as I would allow her
to, and Mrs Sally Betts, after almost sixteen years of per-
plexity and confusion, most bravely borne, has eventually
typed our tenth volume.

My unbounded love and gratitude to them both is here-
with recorded.

D.v.d.B.
London

PART ONE

Chapter 1

It really wasn't the sort of morning on which rotten things are supposed to happen.

All the way up from the little iron gate at the bottom of Great Meadow the larks were singing like anything. The sun was hot and the leaves on the elder and ash at the edge of the gully had just started to turn yellowy-goldish, because it was going to be September in a minute although you would hardly have known it, it was so beautiful.

The high grasses were full of crickets and grasshoppers and the field curved away up towards the sky, soft and smooth and fawn as a deer's back. Only very little clouds drifted in high above from the sea at Cuckmere and sort of got melted away by the warm breeze which came in the other way from the Weald.

We didn't really know much about the witch. We had spoken to her once, years ago, with all her cats round her. She had been quite nice and showed us a sort of shell thing with *Bombay* written on it, which is a town in India, because we had given her a bit of a help with some wood for her fire. But that was all, and she didn't put a spell on us, as far as we knew, although my sister did get the measles a bit later on and I didn't, which was jolly lucky for me. But that was the only time we'd been really close. I mean, we never spoke again or anything like that.

We sometimes used to see her hurrying along, shoulders

all hunched up in a very witchy way, and her old black felt hat pulled down right to her eyes looking exactly like half an egg, which is why we called her Eggshell, although we actually knew that her real name was Nellie Wardle. She never spoke to us, or even looked, and we didn't dare speak to her in case of something funny happening. You couldn't be sure with witches. She just went on past, wagging her head from side to side and muttering awful-sounding things to herself in her long black draggly coat which was really quite green if you saw it in the sunlight, which we didn't often because she mostly came out at dusk. With the bats. Witches do.

We never went back to the caravan on Red Barn Hill where she lived with all those cats, because it was a pretty creepy, lonely sort of place, and if you had been 'spelled' there no one would ever have known about it.

But sometimes we saw her on Fridays when Fred the Fish drove in from Newhaven in his shiny little Morris van. We'd be able to see her quite close to, because after everyone had bought what they wanted, and Fred was clearing up his boxes and the big brass scales, she used to get a fat parcel of fish heads and skin and stuff wrapped up in newspaper which he gave her for her cats.

And that's how we knew that she was dead.

This Friday he was scraping the guts and so on into a bucket, and I was putting our herrings into the red and black shopping-bag, and I said to him, 'Are you saving all those bits for Mrs Wardle's cats?'

'No. No more I don't. She's gorn.' And he went on wiping his chopping-board.

My sister looked very shocked and said, 'Gorn where?' Which would have got her a box on the ears if Lally had heard her. He just shrugged and said, 'Gorn,' again, but he didn't know where for certain.

'There's two places, ain't there?' he said. 'There's your Heaven and there's your Hell. Who can tell where she's skipped to?'

My sister looked quite white and said, 'There's the other place too . . . the Purgatory place, isn't there?'

He wrung out his cloth, squeezed it quite dry and said that was *Life*. Not death. And then we knew that she was dead. Of course, we had really known as soon as he had said, 'Gorn.' I mean we knew it wasn't to Seaford or Hastings or somewhere, but much worse. And further.

But dead. It seemed very final, sort of. We were quite miserable when we went across to Baker's the confectioner's to get Lally her Fry's chocolate bar and us our Sherbert Dabs. Miss Annie said, 'Yes, pore soul, didn't you know? Jack Diplock found her on the path with all her cats sitting round her, dead as the Dodo.' She said she reckoned she'd gorn just in time to get ready for the haunting at the end of October.

But we didn't take much notice of Miss Annie, who was nice but 'not all there', Lally said, ever since she had carried a full pail of petrol from the pump outside the shop into the parlour to sponge out some stains from her father's best suit, in front of the open range.

There was a most terrific bang and Miss Annie and the parlour window and most of the wall and a quite big armchair blew themselves right into the middle of the market square. Which caused a terrible fuss and broke everybody's window as far away as Sloop Lane. She was in the hospital for a very long time and when she came out they said that she had a 'dicky' heart and that her poor head was a bit addled. So we didn't take much notice of what she said really, on account of her being not quite right in the upper storey, as Lally said quite kindly. Anyway, we didn't believe about the haunting part and Hallowe'en. That was soppy.

But it was pretty sad about the witch being dead, especially on such a lovely morning. Of course, we did know about people being dead, but we actually didn't know very many who were. So that made it worse about Nellie Wardle, because we did know her, and had spoken to her even.

We clambered over the rickety iron fence behind the privy, walked down through the vegetable garden, and when we got to the lean-to, a sort of wooden creosoted shed stuck on to the side of the cottage where we kept sacks of potatoes, marrows, long tresses of onions, and all sorts of things we hadn't got room for in the kitchen, we heard Lally's voice quite loudly coming through the open window. She was singing 'Moonlight and Roses', which was one of her two favourites. So we knew she was in a very cheerful mood, and this would make it difficult to tell her the sad news.

She got to the door just as we arrived, with a big stone gallon jar of ginger beer in her arms.

'There you are, then. Dawdling, I'll be bound. It's almost eleven and you've been gone a fortnight.' She shut the lean-to door and we all went into the kitchen. But we hadn't said anything.

The kitchen was very cool and shady with its red brick floor and bumpy whitewashed walls. We put the shopping-bag on the table, and the little list she had written for Mr Wilde, the grocer, and the change from my pocket.

'My word,' she said. 'Mr and Mrs Glum we are. You haven't got into mischief, you two, have you? Speak up if you have or forever hold your peace.'

'No. We haven't got into mischief,' I said. 'But we've got something beastly to tell you.'

'Oh,' she said, standing the big stone jar on the draining-board. 'And what's that then? One of you fell into a cow pat, that it?'

'No. It's not anything like that. But it's very sad, and perhaps you'd better sit down before we tell you.'

'Sit down!' she said, quite crossly but looking a bit worried too. You could see that easily. 'Why should I sit down, pray?'

'Because you might have a turn if you get a shock.'

'You've lost the change from my ten-shilling note?'

'No. It's there, on the table.'

'Well, what is it then? Come along, I haven't got all day.'

'Well . . .' said my sister. 'It's about the witch.'

'What witch?'

'Who lived up in the caravan on Red Barn Hill.'

We thought that would give her bit of an idea, saying '*who lived*'. But it didn't.

'I don't know any witch who lives in any caravan,' said Lally firmly.

'Eggshell,' I said. 'She did.'

'Oh! Nellie Wardle.' She seemed quite relieved and started to unpack the red and black shopping-bag. 'You got the herrings, I am hoping?'

'Yes. And the roes.'

'Soft ones or hard?'

'Soft. He said you liked them better.'

'And so I do, and so do you . . . on toast.' She set the packages on the table and went over to the dresser for a plate. 'What's going to give me a turn, I'd like to know if you don't very much mind, about Nellie Wardle then?'

'She's dead,' I said quickly. 'Jack Diplock found her lying on the path with all her cats round her. Dead.'

'That your sad news then?' She was unwrapping the herrings and slipping them on to the big Lowestoft plate.

'Yes. Don't you think it's sad?'

She lifted the plate to her nose and had a good sniff. 'Fresh as fresh,' she said and covered them with a clean cloth. 'Of course it's sad. Always is when someone is deceased. Very sad. But she passed away weeks ago. That's old news to me.'

'Weeks! Fred the Fish only said today about it.'

'Fred the Fish doesn't live here, does he? Lives over Southease . . . and you don't see him that often.' She started unwrapping the soft roes, and put them into a small pudding basin with a saucer on top and went to the meat-safe on the wall by the sink. 'Mrs Fluke told me when I was in

Wood's last week. It clean slipped my mind. Anyway, it was probably a happy release for the poor soul, all on her own, damp and cold up on that hill. You know what it's like in the fog up there, don't you? And she had no kith or kin . . . just herself.'

'What's kith or kin?' said my sister, pulling up her socks, which had got all runkled from hurrying up the hill.

'Oh. Uncles and aunts. Mothers and fathers. Relations.'

'None?'

'None. No one could find anyone. Beattie Fluke and Doris Pratt went to the churchyard, just for the look of things.'

'What a dreadful thing. To have no one in the whole world when you are dead,' said my sister. 'But I suppose she wouldn't have, would she, if she was really a witch.'

Lally had put the herring roes away in the meat-safe and was washing her hands at the sink. 'Now, let's have no more of this silly business about witches. Nellie Wardle was a poor unhappy old woman, and that's no cause for you to poke fun at her.'

'It's not fun,' I said. 'It's a bit frightening really . . .'

'Stuff and nonsense. You've been got at by the village children. I've told you and told you, they'll fill your head with all kinds of balderdash. Now get from under my feet, I've a busy morning what with young Master Bromley coming in on the six o'clock and your lunch to cook. And I hope you got the currants or no cake for tea.'

Brian Scott Bromley was a bit boring. He was one year

older than me, and his father worked with our father at *The Times*. He was half an orphan because his mother had died one day, so he went to boarding-school, and we didn't really like him very much. But he was coming to stay for a week with us before the summer finished because his father had gone off and married another lady and they had gone to somewhere in France for a holiday, and he was alone. So our mother said come and stay with us at the cottage, we would love it. But we really rather hated it. I mean people staying. You always had to do what *they* wanted, at least if Lally was about, and never what you wanted. It seemed very unfair. And Brian Scott Bromley was a bit showy-offy. And spoke in a very soppy voice, which was, Lally said, because he went to boarding-school, but she thought it was very nice and gentlemanly. We thought it was ghastly, but we had to be a bit nice because he had a secondhand mother, instead of the one he had got used to, and we had both of our parents, which was pretty lucky, except we only had one set of grandparents, which worried my sister very much indeed.

'About kith and kin,' she said, settling herself down beside me under the elderberry bush up by the privy. 'It's a bit muddly. How many *ought* you to have, then?'

'As many as you like. I mean, it doesn't matter. They just happen.'

'But we've only got two grandparents, haven't we, so that's a bit wonky, isn't it. Anyway, they're our mother's and they live in awful Scotland in the mist or something.'

'Our father hasn't got any. Only Granny Nutt, and she doesn't count really.'

'Why?'

'Because she's not really our grandmother, she's our father's aunt. But she just says she's our grandmother so that we don't feel out of it.'

'Out of what?' said my sister, eating a handful of elderberries and spitting the pips out all over my bare knee. So I hit her and she started coughing.

'It's very silly to do that to a person who is eating things. They could choke.'

'Well, you spat all over my knee. Look. Pips everywhere.'

'I don't like the pips. Do you mean our father is a orphan then? These aren't ripe yet.'

'Yes. Except we don't know if his father is dead or not. Just disappeared in the jungle or somewhere. Perhaps he is. Then *he* would be an orphan. And you have to say "an" orphan, not "a".'

'Why?' said my sister.

'I don't know. But you have to. It's the rules.'

'You just make up your own rules. I know. Oh! It's such a rotten day. The witch being dead, Brian Scott Bromley coming to stay, and we haven't got enough kith and kin and I bet you Brian Scott Bromley's new mother is wicked. Bet you.'

'Why should she be?'

'Because she's his stepmother, silly, and stepmothers are. That poor Snow White girl had a dreadful one. And she turned into a witch pretty quickly.'

From the elderberry bush you could see almost all the

back of the cottage and the orchard part. Only it wasn't really an orchard, just about four or five big old trees – and the apples were getting quite red already except for on the Granny Smith, and they never got red, just yellowy-green, and there was a big bunch of mistletoe on one. Lally said we'd have a bit in the house for Christmas, because this year, which was terrifically good, we were going to have Christmas at the cottage, and not in boring old London, for a treat.

I felt quite cheerful thinking of that and I began not to mind Brian Scott Bromley coming, because at least he wasn't coming at Christmas.

'Isn't it funny,' said my sister, undoing her sandal and pulling at her sock, which had got all ruckled under her foot. 'Isn't it funny about Mrs Fluke and Mrs Pratt going to the churchyard?'

'I don't see why. People do at funerals and things.'

'But being a witch, she ought to have been buried at the crossroads, with a huge big wooden stick stuck in her.'

'You heard what Lally said. She isn't a witch. We just made her one.'

'And what about the haunting Miss Annie said about? At Hallowe'en? If they had stuck a stick in her she wouldn't be able to haunt, would she.'

'It's all silly. You know Miss Annie isn't right in the head.'

'The top storey,' said my sister, and pulled off her other sandal. 'Oh dear! I do wish this Brian wasn't coming. I wonder what happened to all her cats?'

I wondered too. There would be no one to feed them

now and that made me feel a bit miserable, especially as Fred the Fish just shoved all the guts and things into a bucket and no one would have taken them to the cats who, probably, were starving. I felt miserable and forgot about Christmas because it was ages and ages away and this was today. And I should have asked him for them for our cat, Minnehaha.

'Perhaps we could go up to the caravan, with Brian Thingummy. And see.'

'See what?' My sister looked quite worried and waved a sock in the air.

'About her cats? If they were all starving or something.'

'I wouldn't dare. I wouldn't simply dare go up there ever again. You can go. With Brian.'

'Well . . .' I said, not feeling very comfortable. 'Perhaps I might then.'

It was shepherd's pie and runner beans for lunch, and Daddies Sauce. Which was a particular treat because it was never allowed in the dining-room when our parents were there, which seemed a pity because it had a quite interesting picture on it of a very happy mother and father and their children, and the father was smiling like anything and holding the bottle of sauce. That's why it was called Daddies, you see. But it was very good sauce anyway, and it went down a treat, as Lally said, with a bit of shepherd's pie. And then there was treacle tart for pudding, only because it was still summertime, and we'd had it hot the day before. We had it cold with clotted cream from the Court Dairy, and it was really pretty good, all sticky and crinkly.

I was quite enjoying everything until Lally said suddenly, 'And I hope you've got the hole dug.'

'Hole?' said my sister making a place with her spoon in the cream so that she could see the treacle on her bit of tart. 'What hole?'

'Don't come the Madam Ostrich with me, my girl. You know very well what hole.'

My sister shrugged, but her mouth was full so she couldn't say anything.

'It's dug,' I said. 'Up by the old bit of flint wall, where we did the last one.'

'And not in the same place, I'm hoping?'

Well she knew it couldn't be in the same place because it would have been pretty awful if it had been, and we wouldn't have been allowed in 'her' kitchen, as she called it. We might not have even had any lunch come to that. And she didn't really think that it was, because she was licking her spoon, not taking much notice. Except, had we dug the hole. Well, *we* had. I had, anyway.

Every Friday night, just as it was getting dark, we had to go up to the privy and cart away the big bucket of Night Soil. That's what it was called, but my sister called it the Bindie Bucket, which was her name for it, and if Lally heard us use it we got a box on the ears all right. We would push a big thick stick under the handle, lift it out of the privy, and hump it across the vegetable garden to the 'hole', which had to be dug earlier in a special place.

If our parents were staying with us, when our father had his holiday from *The Times*, which wasn't very long, he used to do it . . . but if we were just with Lally we had to. And it was pretty rotten, I can tell you.

We always had to do it in the dark, which was terribly silly because there was no one for miles and miles who could have seen us. And anyway, who would want to watch somebody emptying their privy? But our parents said it had to be done at night, and so at night it was. Because it was correct, or something. And because it was dark it was doubly difficult on account of we had to have a hurricane lamp to see the way. It was jolly difficult to hold on to the big pole with one hand and the hurricane lamp with the other to see that you didn't fall over the rhubarb or trip over the bean-sticks, because if you did it would have been pretty terrible, and I always had to lead. So we were extra careful.

'While I'm drying up, after supper, you two nip off with the lamp and I'll keep young Brian here by me: he can help me with the drying. Can't have your Guest running about with the Night Soil, can we?'

'Why ever not?' said my sister, scraping her plate quite hard.

'If you go on doing that very much longer, Madde-moselle, you'll have the pattern off. Leave over, do! Such manners I've never seen.'

'But why can't he?' said my sister. 'He's a boy and I'm a girl.'

'Goodness me today!' cried Lally. 'Of course he can't. He's hardly been in the house a couple of minutes. It's *our* business, not his.'

My sister made a terrible choking noise and covered her

face with her napkin. Lally went quite red in the face when I started to snort and pushed my hand over my mouth.

'And pray what's given us all the hysterics, may I ask?' said Lally getting redder than ever. She did if she felt she had said something funny without knowing.

'Business has,' said my sister and almost fell off her chair. Lally gave her a terrific box on the ears and told us to mind our p's and q's and help her clear the table. But you could see she was a bit angry with herself for making us laugh and not really knowing why. That's what made us laugh all the more, so she sent us out into the garden until we could behave ourselves.

'I've got the hiccups,' said my sister, 'because of the Bindie Bucket . . . Anyway, one thing, she said No Baths tonight because of this Brian person. So that's good.'

'Unless we spill it,' I said. 'Then we'd have to, wouldn't we?'

'Don't say! It might happen. But it's good about no bath, isn't it.'

Every Friday we had to have our baths. First of all we had to go wooding to get enough sticks and stuff to keep the copper really hot, and that used to start just after washing up lunch. Well, first of all, before the wooding even started, I had to get the water up from the pump. Buckets and buckets to fill the copper, and it was huge. So big that when the wooden lid was on we used to stand the two Primus stoves on the top, and the little paraffin oven where Lally did her cooking if we weren't using the range. Which we didn't much, in the summer. So you can see it was pretty hard to fill. There was a small firehole underneath, and that had to be filled with the wood all afternoon. So it was water in the top and wood in the bottom part.

Then we had to get the big tin bath out of the lean-to, and dust it round, and stand it on a big piece of linoleum on the bricks in front of the copper fire. Then there was the clothes-horse standing there with towels around it for airing, and also to keep off any draughts, the big bar of pink Lifebuoy soap, and the old loofah: and then we could have our baths.

First my sister, because she was the youngest, and when she was finished we topped it up with fresh hot water from the copper, because it was getting a bit cool by this time. I had mine while they went into the sitting-room and had cocoa and alphabet biscuits.

So you can see it was rather a lot of work. And even when I had had my bath there was more, because we had to half-empty the bath by bucket and saucepan, pouring it down the sink. Then Lally used to drag the bath to the kitchen door and tip it down the big drain, and all the steam went up in the air like clouds.

So it was a pretty busy sort of time. It wouldn't have done with a Guest to entertain, so that's why we were not having baths. Which was fearfully good. Our father had one this way once – but only once, because he tipped it over and the kitchen was flooded and the fire went out and Lally had a turn. He said he'd caught a chill and would rather be dirty, but we know that he

went down to the Star in the village and had his there. So
did our mother. It really was a bit more sensible, but Lally
was braver and had hers, and we used to sit in the sitting-
room and hear her singing, la, la, la, and splashing about
and it sounded very nice and happy.

So, you see, Friday was really rather a busy day,
and especially this time because we were alone with
Lally: our father had had his holiday and gone back to
The Times, and our mother went with him to London for
company. But we just stayed for two more weeks
and then it was back to dreadful school, only, we didn't
think of that so as not to spoil the last days. Except Brian
Scott Bromley would do that anyway, so what was the
use?

He wasn't really so awful as a matter of fact. I mean,
not like Alice McWhirter, who only had a father and was
really awful. But he was pretty funny and used very difficult words which even Lally couldn't understand. When
he arrived on the six o'clock bus he was wearing his school
uniform, with his cap on, and lace-up shoes, and we
thought that was pretty peculiar for a holiday. Lally said,
'Shush,' when we mentioned it to her and that he hadn't
settled down with his new mother and that it all took
time.

He had sandy-reddish hair and a very pale face,
glasses and red lips, and got up at the table every
time that Lally did, even to get a spoon from the
drawer, until she told him not to, very nicely. We
thought that perhaps he was going to be sick or wanted
to be excused or something, but she said it was just
manners and a pity we hadn't learnt some, but perhaps

a few of his might brush off on us. Which we hoped they wouldn't because good manners seemed pretty exhausting.

Chapter 2

The next day he looked a bit better because he had on a pair of shorts and a shirt, but still the lace-up shoes. He seemed to quite enjoy coming with us to see all our favourite places, like the gully and the smugglers' cave up near Windover Hill, only he said it wasn't one, but 'in all probability' was part of the old windmill, or had been a store for 'ammunition' during the Great War. You see, these were the sorts of words he used: 'probability' and 'ammunition' and lots more. And he read rather grown-up books like *Ivanhoe*, which I thought was very dense, but he liked the river part where we took him, and even helped my sister pick a few waterlilies, the little yellow ones. He didn't seem to mind very much when his lace-up shoes got all muddy, although he did say, quite loudly, 'Oh! Hells bells!' Which we thought pretty interesting.

'I'm not quite sure what to call the woman at your house,' he said when we were walking up from the river.

'What woman?' said my sister.

'Well . . . the only one there. She cooks, and we had supper and so on last night and she asked me to help with the drying-up. That one.'

'Oh. That's just Lally.'

'But who is she? I mean, what's her name?'

'Lally,' said my sister. 'She looks after us.'

'But she isn't Miss or Mrs Lally, is she?'

'No. Lally. That's all. We couldn't say nanny when we were little so it got stuck at Lally. That's all she is.'

'Your *nanny*?' said Brian Scott Bromley, wiping his muddy shoes on a big clump of dock leaves. 'How infinitely quaint.'

'She *was* our nanny. Until we grew up,' I said.

He looked at me very strangely, and made a funny laughing noise. 'I see. But what should I call her? I can't call her Lally, she's not *my* nanny. I never had one.'

'Well,' said my sister. 'Her mother and father are called Mr and Mrs Jane and I think her real name is Ellen, but I don't know. I heard Mrs Jane call her that once when she was cross about something. But usually it's just Lally.'

'I'll call her Miss Jane. That would be perfectly correct, I'm certain.'

'She'll be rather surprised if you do.'

'Well, I mean, one has to be decent about this sort of thing. The woman has a name and it seems to me correct to use it. I don't know her familiarly, do I?'

'I don't know,' I said, not knowing really, and being a bit worried by the grown-up sort of speaking.

'Well, of course I don't. First time I clapped eyes on her was yesterday evening when we got in from the bus. She seems a decent sort of person, so I would like to behave correctly. I think it very demeaning not to give her her proper station.'

We walked up, crossed the road, pushed open the iron gate into Great Meadow and started the climb up to the cottage. But we didn't say very much, because we didn't really know what to say to Brian Scott Bromley. My sister crossed her eyes at me, when he wasn't looking, and put a finger to her head, meaning that she thought he was a bit wonky. Which I was beginning to think too. But I pretended not to notice what she was doing in case he saw. And so she just clumped ahead singing any-sort-of-song and holding her khaki shorts up by pushing her hands into the pocket because they were too big really for her, and she had broken her snake-belt when she fell out of a tree when we were picking sloes.

Just as we got to the beginning of the gully, I said to Brian Thingummy that it might be quite interesting for him to see the smugglers' way to the cottage, instead of walking up Great Meadow, which was in the blazing sun, and the gully was shady and cool, and he said, 'Very well.' So we slid down a chalky slope under the trees, and heard my sister scream out in the field on top.

It was quite a terrible scream, three very loud 'Eeeee!' s.

'What's the matter then?' I called out through the tangle of ivy and roots from the bottom of the gully.

'You're vile!' she shrieked. So I knew she wasn't dead or bitten by an adder or something. Just furious. 'How do you know the stallion isn't loose in the field? It may be, but you don't care. Oh no! Just leave me alone here and disappear down the gully. You're a stinking beast.'

'What's the matter with her?' said Brian Thing, pushing in his shirt where it had come out all bumfley from his shorts because of sliding down the chalk slope, which was the only way you could get into the gully because it was so over-grown.

'I think it's because of Aleford's stallion. She is frightened it might trample her to death or something.'

'Most unlikely,' said Brian. 'I mean, unless she provoked it.'

I didn't know what he really meant, so I didn't say anything, and anyway she was coming down the slope and making a dreadful clattering noise scrabbling under the bramble and ivy.

'Some people are so rotten,' she said. 'I could have easily been frightened to death up there, all alone. In a field full of stallions.'

'You don't know it's there,' I said.

'You don't know it *isn't* there,' she said as we pushed through trailing old man's beard. 'Don't you think this is very nice indeed, Brian?' she said, as if she had made the gully all by herself. So I quickly put that right – she was such a show-off.

'The smugglers made it,' I said. 'Years ago. And they used to smuggle brandy and all manner of things down from the little church at the top of Great Meadow. It was their secret way to the village, you see.' I felt quite pleased – *that* shut her up a bit.

But then he said, with that squinty smile, 'I very much doubt it. I think it was just a downland track which went up from the main road to the windmill at the top, beyond your cottage. You showed it me last evening.'

'Our mother fell through the floor once, in the cottage, and landed in a terrible spooky cave thing right under the house, and they said it was an old smugglers' cave and was part of a tunnel which came all the way from the church,' said my sister. 'That's what they said. And they should know, they're grown up, after all.'

'Quite a decent idea,' said Brian Beastly. 'But I'd take it with a pinch of salt.'

'It is the smallest church in England,' said my sister. 'We'll take you there if you like? Unless you are an un-goddy sort of person. Are you?'

'I don't think it *is* the smallest church. From what my

father told me it's only a fragment of a much larger building. And it's not the smallest in England. I rather believe
that is in the north somewhere.'

We walked along in silence for a bit. I mean, he did
rather put you off all the time and it was quite hard not to
give him a good bonk on the nose, only he was a bit
bigger than me, and wore glasses. So I thought I would
just change the subject and asked him if he had managed
all right in his room when he went to bed.

'Managed what?' he said quite nicely, stooping under a
huge tangle of bramble, which frightened a thrush so that
it clattered off scolding.

'Well, last evening. You know, with your po. Chamber
pot,' I said, seeing he didn't seem to know.

And he laughed sort of and said, 'Oh thanks, yes, managed all right. I didn't have to use the chamber pot thing.'

'It's the Guest's one,' said my sister. 'It's got a pheasant
on the bottom.'

'I just piddled out the window,' said Brian Thing.

'Out the window?' I said.

'Well . . . only once.'

'The ginger beer,' said my sister. 'But how rude to do it
out of the window. Just suppose Lally had been walking
underneath.'

'It was quite late, and I heard her saying goodnight to
you both from her room, so I was quite safe.'

'And right into the apple trees! I'll never eat an apple off
those trees ever again. And it'll stain the tiles, I bet.'

Brian looked very huffy, and his white face went quite
red. 'It didn't go anywhere near the wretched apple trees.
They're miles away.'

'Well ... I do think it's very rude, especially when you've got your own po.'

We got to the end of the gully near the rubbish tip of old cans and bits of bedstead, and then we scrambled up the slope and the cottage was in front of us, all shimmering in the sun and behind it you could see the big clump of elm trees where the little church was.

'If you don't believe in smugglers, we have a witch's house we could show you,' said my sister, feeling quite brave again now that she was so near the cottage and could see Lally in her pinafore walking down the path past the lean-to. 'She's "gorn", though, so you won't see her, but he' – she jerked her head at me as we started to climb over the rickety iron fence – 'he could show you where she lived. It's very creepy, and there are millions of cats everywhere.'

Brian looked a bit startled and his shirt had come out again, so he tucked it back. But he didn't say anything, so you could see he was a bit impressed by the idea of a witch's house, even though it was just a caravan. But we didn't say that.

'If you'd like to come and see it, I'll take you. It's not far from here. About two miles along the Downs.'

'Very kind,' he said. But he was still looking at us in a peculiar way, as if we were dotty or something.

Really. People are funny.

'Brian!' said Lally in surprise. 'Where have they taken you? Your good shoes caked in mud! I declare, I can't turn my back on you two without you go and do something underhand. Give them to me. Come along, take them off, it's a fine summer's day, you'll come to no grief on the grass in your socks. Give them to me and I'll clean them up in a trice, otherwise it cakes. Chalk does.'

She was being very bossy but you could see Brian didn't want a bit to take his shoes off, only he knew he had to, and you could see why when he did: there were huge holes in his socks. My sister was just about to say something about the holes – I mean, you could see that, and she had pointed – when Lally gave her a box on the ears, not very hard, and said, 'Into the kitchen with you, Maddemoselle, and wash your hands . . . Fifteen minutes to lunchtime.'

We walked behind her to the cottage.

'What's for lunch, then?' I said, because there was a bit of a silence and I thought Brian Thing was a bit pale looking at all his toes. Almost.

'Tea, toast and six eggs,' said Lally quite crossly and went into the kitchen with the shoes.

'It isn't really that,' I said. 'It's just what she always says when you ask tea, toast and six eggs. It's to put you off and stop you being a Nosey Parker, I think.'

But he didn't say anything, just looked rather uncomfortable, and suddenly Lally stuck her head out of the kitchen window. 'Don't loll about there, you two, wash your hands and show Brian where. And, Brian? – why don't you take off your socks and go barefoot? It's such a hot day, and I'm doing my wash this afternoon. You're bound to have got them muddy . . . hurry along. And you two take off *your* sandals – I don't want you traipsing about my kitchen with mud everywhere, thank you very much. Lunch in ten minutes . . .'

Well, it was pretty silly telling us to take off our sandals because she never did before and they weren't even muddy, but she did it just to make old Brian Thing feel at home, on account of he must have felt a bit silly sitting there on the grass in his holey socks. So we did and he did, and it was rather a nice feeling putting your feet into the grass and walking on the red bricks in the kitchen, and he seemed to quite cheer up. And so did I because it was my favourite lunch anyway: pressed tongue and pickled onions and damson tart for afterwards. It was quite funny really, because old Brian Thing quite forgot about his shoes and his holey socks, and he also forgot to say Miss Jane once. He just said Lally. Like we did.

In the end it really wasn't such a bad week. Well, as weeks go. It's always a bit mouldy if you have a Guest and have to be extra polite to him and do everything he wants to do and make him feel welcome. Even Family Hold Back on the pudding and so on, which was a bit irritating.

And Brian Thing got quite nice, well, as nice as anyone can who looks like that: all pale and speckled and wearing tin glasses. But Lally kept on saying, 'Just you both remember he's got something to worry about with a new mother and all, and he's a well-educated boy and not used to people like you.' And that put us in our places, or so she jolly well thought. But anyway, we were all right to him and he wasn't bad. And he got better after the holey socks time, and especially after the next day when Lally came down with us all to the village – which was a bit funny because she never came down in the mornings and always told us to skedaddle from under her feet and find something to do or go for the messages while she whipped round the house, as she called it.

They were quite surprised in Wilde's, the grocer's, too. And bossy Miss Maltravers behind the post office counter-place said, 'Well! Miss Jane. As I breathe! What a surprise. We don't often see you here of a morning.'

'No more you don't,' said Lally. 'Better things to do than traipsing about the shops, Miss Maltravers. Bit of elbow grease up at the top of the hill, that's what. But now and again I like to keep my eye on things, otherwise you get taken for granted, and as a matter of fact I want a shilling postal order if you please.' While Miss Maltravers was looking for it in her book, Lally said, really quite loudly in front of two or three people we didn't even know, 'Mr Wilde, by the by, that Cheddar you sent up with the children last week was dry as dry. Australian, I shouldn't wonder, and made the journey all the way on the open deck by the look of it, and you know we always take English. So next time you haven't got it in, send up a nice piece of Leicester, will you. No fobbing off, Mr Wilde.' And he looked a bit grumpy and said he was very sorry he was sure. And then, looking up at the ceiling of the shop which was hung with legs of ham, kettles and lids, saucepans, wooden spoons in bundles and tin mugs with *Poland* printed on their bottoms, as well as lots of fly-papers on account of all the flies and wasps which buzzed about because of the sugar and currants in the big wooden drawers behind the counter, Lally said, 'I wonder if you have such a thing as a pair of plimsolls as'll fit this young gentleman here.' She put her hand on Brian Thing's head to show she didn't mean me. And Mr Wilde, who was wrapping up some bacon which he'd just sliced, said yes, he thought so, and they were ninepence ha' penny a pair.

What was funny was that she paid for them out of her own purse and not the housekeeping one, which was different and had a handle. It didn't leave very much in it, because when she paid Miss Maltravers for the postal order she did it with a sixpence and some coppers, and when she shook her little purse nothing rattled in it.

Anyway, Brian Thing got his plimsolls, which were better than his lace-ups in the country, and he seemed very pleased and asked if he could carry the red and black shopping-bag. That was really my job, but Lally said yes, so I couldn't say anything because he was a Guest and all. I felt it was a bit Teacher's Pet sort of thing but remembered about kith and kin and him only having half, if you know what I mean, with a new mother who told him to call her 'Kathleen', he said.

When we got to the long white bridge over the Cuckmere the tide was coming in and there were two swans dobbling about by the far bank with three cygnets, but we didn't stay looking at them for long because the cob started stretching out his neck and making rather grumpy hissing noises and flapping his wings, and my sister hurried across the bridge and you could hear Brian Thing's feet going plonk plonk plonk on the wooden boards. At the little bridge over the stream where we used to catch roach sometimes, for Minnehaha our cat, Lally suddenly said, 'Pouf. But it's hot! Let's all have a sit down here in the shade for a couple of ticks. Brian, you can change into your plimsolls, and I've got a quarter of Liquorice Allsorts, who wants one?'

Brian changed his shoes, and we all had a Liquorice Allsort, but only one because of not spoiling our appetites.

And Lally fished about in the red and black bag and took out an envelope and pushed in the postal order; then licked the flap and stuck it down.

'Now,' she said, 'we must get a move on. I'm behind with my work and you'll get no lunch this morning if we aren't quick sharp up the hill.' She bustled about with her bags and purses and we all clambered up to the main road and had a good look right and left, because you never knew if there was a motor car coming or not, although there hardly ever was.

Then we all ran very quickly across the main road to the little iron gate by the barn which led into Great Meadow and all sort of collided and Lally said, 'Drat the thing.' The envelope fell on the road and I saw that it said 'Miss Gladys Cooper's Beauty Treatment, 121A Hampstead Road, London', and so I just picked it up and gave it to her, and she looked a bit funny and said, 'Nosey Parker.' I said I wasn't, so she said, 'Well now that you've got it, put it in the post box,' because there was one stuck on a wooden post by the gate with 'ER VII' in curly red letters. So I did.

'Can you see any cows?' she said as we opened the creaky gate. But there weren't any, and anyway they were usually Aleford's heifers and not cows, only, she said that didn't make tuppence worth of difference to her, cows were cows, whatever you liked to call them and she'd rather go round by road than up the field and be trampled to death by those great things.

'They'd run away if you just shook your fist at them,' said Brian Thing.

'Would they indeed,' said Lally. 'And me in my red and

white polka dot? Drive them mad it would. Shake my
fist! Bet you've never been surrounded by a whole herd of
them, have you? All snuffling and thumping the grass,
with those huge eyes, and they lower their heads and get
ready to charge you. I know. I was caught like that once,
wasn't I?'

'She had a terrible turn,' said my sister. 'So would I
have.'

'Just up the top. I saw them right down almost at the
Court and the faster I went the faster they came until they
were all round me. *Terrible* it was. Enough to turn you
white.'

'She had to have smelling-salts,' said my sister. 'In a
little green bottle, and it makes your eyes stingy.'

'It's ammonia,' said Brian Thing.

'Whatever it is,' said Lally, 'I had to have it.'

'Smells just like wet beds,' said my sister and ran up the
hill because she knew she'd have got a box on the ears for
that.

'Take no notice,' Lally said. 'Best ignore that kind of
behaviour, I'll deal with Maddemoselle myself later. Running wild the two of them ... I don't know. And me
responsible. And by the by,' she said suddenly turning to
me, 'if you're wondering why I didn't send my letter
from the post office but from the box by the gate, and I
am as sure as sure you are, it's because I don't want Miss
Maltravers knowing where I send my letters to. She's a
terrible gossip, that woman, she's got a tongue like the
clapper of a bell, all over the place, any bit of news she
spreads it. So that's why.'

'Was it secret then? The letter?'

''Course not. Secret! Whatever next. Private, that's all,'
she said. 'And you just M.Y.O.B.'

Meaning 'Mind Your Own Business'. So I thought that
was pretty interesting to tell my sister a bit later on. If I
could remember the lady's name.

The lane beside the Star Inn ran right up on to the Downs. If
you went all the way up you would pretty soon come to
Long Burgh, which was about the top really. From there
you could look all round you and see everywhere, as if it was
all your own. Far down, at the bottom, was the village, and
quite far away was Alciston and Berwick, and then the river
wavering through the valley all silvery in the sun. Past that
you could see our house and the church in the trees and right
on to Windover Hill. There was never any noise up there,
just the larks going twittering up in the sky, and the wind
coming in from the sea where it was all golden and blue, and
across it, I mean really miles away so that you couldn't tell,
was France. Brian Thing said that he had been there once
and that it was quite decent except they ate terrible mucked-
up food. So I didn't say anything, because I rather liked
mucked-up food . . . anyway, French mucked-up.

We were going to see the witch's caravan, because it
was his last day and I was a bit curious, and wondering
about all the cats and so on. But he wasn't very keen, he
said, but was being polite anyway, so it didn't matter.

'What would you do,' I said, 'if you actually saw one?
A witch. What then?'

'What would I do?'

'Yes. If suddenly, just coming out of that wood there,
hoppity, skippity, an old black witch came?'

He laughed, but it sounded like a bit of a sniff really. 'Always presupposing that I believed in them, which I don't, I'd say, "Good-day," and that's all.'

He really made you feel quite rotten, all those words, he was terribly stuck-up and Londony. I quite went off him when he spoke like that, but otherwise he was all right, I suppose.

'I expect it's because you live in London, and don't believe in things like that. Of course I don't suppose you could have witches in a city really, but you can in the country. We've got lots here in Sussex. They do spells, you know, and sometimes they kidnap children and sell them to the gypsies. Mrs Fluke, who's lived here all her life, had a spell put on her by this witch to stop her chilblains. And it worked. So there. She told me.'

'I think someone's pulling your leg,' he said, and ran on up the hill to show that he could. Without getting out of breath. Only, when I got up to him he was. And quite red in the face too, which served him right.

Where he was standing there was a little break of twisty elder bushes, all bent by the winds, and just below, the track from the village faded away into scrubby grass and chalk ruts, and there, all by itself looking very creepy and forlorn, was the caravan. But there were no cats anywhere and it looked, from where we were, very closed up. The little tin chimney with the pointy top was all rusty and the pink and blue paint was grey now, and all peeling off.

'That's it,' I said in a whisper because it seemed a whisper sort of place, like church or a museum. Because she was dead, I suppose.

'It's a caravan,' said Brian Thing. 'How ever did they get it up here, I wonder?'

'I suppose with a horse, but years ago, because the shafts are all broken, look.'

And they were, just lying rotten in the grass.

'Where's the cauldron then?' he said with a twisty smile.

'I don't know,' I said. 'But there's an old milk churn over there.'

'Witches always have cauldrons, to do their spells round. They boil up toads and newts and things and make a brew. And curse people. Didn't you know?' He was smiling in a very sarcastic manner so I was just about to say, 'Well . . . let's go back now . . .', when there was a very strange thing. The closed shutter slowly, slowly, creaked open. We looked at it. I didn't breathe. Then the other one did. And there was no noise, just the creak and then stillness. And there was no wind so it wasn't that. Then suddenly there was a dreadful little 'bonk! bonk! bonk!' noise. It was quite clear. And it was coming from the tin chimney stack. From *inside* it. And just as I was going to start back into the elder bushes there was a terrific noise of ghostly rattling and the pointy tin lid flew off, right up in the air. So I just turned and ran, and Brian Thing came with me, and his face was quite white now – only, his ears were red. And just as we pushed into the bushes there was a terrible noise from the caravan. 'Wooooo! Wooooo!' it went, very high and wavery, like an owl but louder, 'Woooo! Woooo!' And Brian Thing said, 'Hells bells,' to himself and was running far ahead of me when there was a most fearful explosion. And I just turned quickly enough to see an old iron stove come sailing out from where the front door of the caravan must have been, and it exploded, sort of, in the grass. And I was so astonished that I tripped

The Caravan.

over a twisty root and as I was getting up there was a booming loud voice yelling, 'Come 'ere you two sneaky barstards,' and it was Reg Fluke and his best friend Perce. So I felt quite silly, but not nearly as silly as Brian Thing, who had almost got down to the village by this time, with his glasses off.

'Wot you up to, then?' said Reg. He was standing on the steps of the caravan and Perce was leaning out of the little window. 'Couple of sneaks.'

So I told them, and Brian Thing came dragging back, and we all looked at each other, and Reg said, 'Stinks terrible inside. You want to smell it?'

So we went up to the caravan and it was all ruined inside, with bits of old rag and papers everywhere. The roof had a huge hole in it which I hadn't noticed before, but there was nothing inside really. Reg had chucked the stove out anyway, but there was an old frying-pan, all rusty, and a little glass-fronted door hanging on its hinges, and more old rags and a torn mattress, and on a wall a cardboard picture of a lot of people sitting in rows, like a school group, with a big ivy-covered house in the back, only, it was quite hard to see because it was all mouldy. And that was all.

'I reckon someone's been through this before, and more than once. Probably come up here and do a bit of snogging from the village, I shouldn't wonder.'

I didn't know what he meant, and anyway it was terrifically smelly and sad looking and there were no cats, and it did stink rather of them. So we all got out and Perce started kicking away at a big log under one of the front wheels.

'Wouldn't take much to shift this,' he said.

'And do what?' I said.

'Shove it down the hill, why not?'

'I don't think we should, it's not our property,' said Brian Thing suddenly speaking for the first time.

'Coo. 'Ark at 'im! Toff-talk! "Not our property" indeed! Don't belong to no one anyway. No kith and kin she didn't 'ave,' said Perce and started really kicking the log. Then Reg started at the other, and they got a bit of tree branch and started to bang about with it. The caravan started shaking all over, and then bits fell off it, and the shutters closed and opened like eyes, and it felt awful really . . . like a person struggling sort of. But they got the two big logs rolled away so that the rickety caravan stood just tilted at the top of the track, and you could see it wouldn't take much to send it down the hill.

It was quite an exciting feeling suddenly, and when Reg yelled at us two to come and help we just went and did what he said. The four of us all pushed very hard at the back part and it started shaking and wobbling and groaning and Reg kept yelling, 'Shove!' So we shoved like anything and suddenly it went away . . . just like that. Everyone jumped aside and the caravan started to rumble very slowly down the track, hit a bump somewhere, and went high up over it. A bit of the roof fell away, and then the whole thing went clattering and crumbling down the track and exploded into a mass of wood and wheels and the tin chimney stack when it hit the chalky bank at the bottom. Then everything was quiet except for the sound of the larks and somewhere a sheep bell going 'tonkle tonkle', which made Perce a bit worried because he suddenly said,

'We best be off then . . . ruddy old shepherd about somewhere,' and he and Reg started running down the track,
laughing and waving their arms in the air. When they got
to the wreck of the caravan he picked up a long piece of
broken pink-painted wood, waving it over his head like a
cricket bat, and they disappeared into the woods.

'I think that was a pretty foul thing to do,' said Brian
Thing.

'But you did it,' I said. 'When they said, "come and
shove," you did.'

'Yes,' he said. 'I know. Part of me wanted to and another
part didn't. Do you know what I mean?'

'Yes,' I said. I did but I didn't . . . and I felt a bit sad
myself, but after all it was all falling down anyway, and
terribly smelly, and she was dead and had no kith or kin
to claim it. So I just wandered down the hill to the ruins
and poked in them with a stick, and underneath a long bit
of stripy rag stuff I found a curious round thing. And the
really funny point was that it was the big spotted shell
with open lips and Bombay written on it which she had
showed us years ago when we helped her with some wood.
So I took it. Because perhaps she would have liked me to
take it and not leave it lying all alone up on the Downs,
because she had taken care of it and showed it to us as a
special treat. Her son had sent it to her. But he was dead.
No kith or kin.

We walked slowly down the track just as the sheep
came spilling over the ridge above us, all baaing and skitter-
ing with skinny legs. They started nibbling away at the
place where the caravan had stood, and the big sheep dog
lifted his leg on the rusty milk churn which was lying on

its side in the grass . . . and Mr Dick, the shepherd, waved to us and went on with his flock. It was as if no one ever had seen the witch, or known that her caravan had stood there. It was a rather sad feeling. So I just held the shell to my chest and we went on home.

Chapter 3

The very first sign of all that it was about to be Christmas was when Lally took down the big mixing-bowl and she and our mother started to make the pudding. It took a long time because all the fruit had to be cut up into little bits, and my sister and I had to de-seed the sultanas that had been steeping in warm rum, which was fearfully boring even though we were allowed to eat a few, without making pigs of ourselves, as they said.

Then it all got lumped together, somehow, by our mother, who was very particular about that part, and everybody had to have a stir with the wooden spoon for luck. The best moment of all was when we scattered the lucky charms into the mixture. They were made of silver, because otherwise you had to wrap them in a titchy bit of paper and you could quite easily swallow them unknowing and they'd pass right through you, Lally said, and then you wouldn't have any luck in the New Year – which was what it was all about.

There was a thimble, and if you got that it meant you'd be a spinster, and a button, which if you found it meant that you'd be a bachelor, and a pig for greed, and a horseshoe for extra luck and so on. And best of all two threepenny pieces which were real silver and boiled and polished so there weren't any germs or anything. And then we all stirred each once more.

It took ages and smelled lovely and we didn't see it again until Christmas Day, which was years away. Well, a long time, because our mother always made the pudding in October, and it was kept in a dark place to get ripe.

That was the first sign. But it was so early that sometimes we forgot all about Christmas until the next sign, which was The Photograph.

Every year our father had a special half-page photograph taken somewhere very beautiful in the snow for the Christmas edition of *The Times*. Quite near the time he would be fussing about like anything about where there was a good fall of snow that year. Or even a really heavy hoar-frost would do, because the picture had to have snow, or anyway a very wintry feeling about it for Christmas. But the trouble was, it didn't always snow at that time, and he got into a terrible fuss and kept on telephoning people all over the British Isles asking them how their snow was. And quite often there wasn't. And that made him very jumpy indeed so he kept on sending his photographers everywhere just to sit and wait until something happened. And they got jolly fed up, they said, sitting about in the Pennines or up in the Shetlands or down in Land's End, because nothing much ever happened, and if it did it wasn't enough.

But sometimes, if we were down at the cottage for a weekend, and it suddenly got very frosty, he'd rush down to the village and telephone The Office to get someone down quick sharp before it all went away and the weather changed.

We were sometimes allowed to go out with him when this happened, which wasn't very often because Sussex was too mild, he said, and we usually went with a very nice photographer we called Uncle Bill. Of course, he wasn't really an uncle, not kith and kin or anything, but we had known him for ever and ever – anyway, long before my sister was born even – and we liked him very much and he was called Mr Warhurst. Well, such a fussing. We went off in the O.M. with cameras and tripods and maps and things, and climbed hills, stamped through woods and went to quite far places like Herstmonceux, where there was a beautiful castle, or Ashdown Forest, or Rye. Wherever we found 'somewhere suitable' we'd stop and have a terrific picnic with Thermos flasks of hot tea or soup, sausage rolls, meat pies, or cold chicken and hard boiled eggs, and wait for the light to be right. We always had to do this. It never seemed to be just right when we got there. And all the time we were eating or drinking they were looking at the sky through little glass things and shouting numbers at each other and looking for the cloud to be just exactly right – there had to be clouds too, that was very important, because you just had to have them with the sun slanting through. The readers liked that, my father said, especially if they were miles away in places like Africa or India or Ceylon or somewhere very far, and in all the heat, and among all the black men, the photograph would remind them of England.

When the light was exactly right there was a terrific rushing about and sometimes my sister and I had to go and actually be in the picture to give it 'interest'. Only, never our faces or fronts, just our backs, and we'd have to drag a big log about, or perhaps carry a heavy bundle of twigs, through the frost or the snow. It was really quite exciting in a way. Anyway, it was for them. My sister got a bit fed up dragging bits of wood about and got cold, and started moaning. I got a bit tired with it all too, but remembered the poor people being terribly hot in Africa or India and in a way that cheered me up. And it cheered us both up to remember that The Photograph was the second sign, which was rather good because it reminded us, you see, of the first sign, the pudding. And that meant Christmas was on its way. Which was even better.

Of course, about the pudding time we started to save up for presents, which was a bit boring to begin with, but quite nice when you got to the shopping part. I mean, it was boring to have to put half your pocket money – and we only got fourpence each a week – into an empty Vim tin to buy other people things. But it had to be done, so we did it. It was quite a good feeling when the tin got heavier and you began to think what you'd buy everyone. The trouble was that you couldn't buy people what *you* wanted. You had to buy them what *they* wanted. And Lally, or our mother, was very particular about that when we came to the shopping part. I didn't know *why* our father wouldn't have liked a very pretty glass goldfish in a little bowl, with waterlilies painted round it, but our mother said he'd detest it, and much prefer a pair of dull old socks. So I just let them choose in the end. You really couldn't fight them. My sister wanted to buy a rather nice little clockwork bird for Lally, which wound up and went rushing about pecking things, but she had to get her a stupid bottle of bath salts in the end. It wasn't worth fighting, you see. Nothing we really liked was 'suitable', they said.

Of course the main thing about Christmas was the presents. We knew it was about the day that Jesus was born and everything, and the presents were supposed to be the ones the kings all brought to the manger that time, but we got a bit muddly about Santa Claus, who seemed quite different from holy things. And it was quite hard to understand. Anyway, it didn't matter much because I knew, ages ago, it wasn't Santa Claus but our father, because I watched one night and saw him creep in and put the stockings at the end of our bed. And years ago, when we were really quite small, Lally took us for the day to Mrs Jane's at Walnut Cottage and, as a special treat, we went to Bentalls in Kingston to see the Goblins' Grotto and Father Christmas. It was a bit worrying because we had seen him at Selfridge's the week before – only, he was at the North Pole there. We stood in a long line waiting to have a word with him, and when it was my sister's turn she went rather red in the face, and he put her on his knee and was being quite decent to her when she suddenly hit him and screamed and screamed so that Lally and Mrs Jane had to rush and take her away. She sobbed and snivelled all the way through the lampshade department and even through the corset one. It was awful really. And people kept turning round.

We went down in the lift and when we got to soft furnishings Lally made us sit down, dried my sister's eyes and asked what on earth was all the fuss about.

'He had terrible red eyes!' said my sister.

'Nonsense!' said Lally. 'Red eyes indeed.'

'Red . . .' she wailed. 'And awful long whiskers and he

made rumbling noises at me and said if I hadn't been a good child in the year he'd come down the chimney and sort me out.'

It took a long time to get her all right, and they only did it at the ABC tea shop when Lally let her have first choose of the cakes. So then she shut up. But we never mentioned Santa Claus again really. And every time she saw one, and there seemed to be hundreds everywhere, she grabbed Lally's hand and hid herself in her skirts. She was very relieved that we had a gas fire in the nursery so he couldn't get down the chimney anyway.

So we knew that presents really came from family and from kind people we knew.

Because we hadn't much kith and kin of our own, we had to invent uncles and aunts, which was quite good in a way because you only had the ones you really liked as uncle or aunt. The rest you just called Mr or Mrs and they didn't count.

Of course, we did have some real kith and kin up in Scotland, who belonged to our mother, but we didn't see them often because they lived so far away in the cold and mists, and although they were quite nice, I suppose, they weren't a bit like us. The one bad mark against them was the presents they sent, and they were awful. I mean, you always knew exactly what the present was long before you even opened it.

Flat.

Just flat.

No lovely bumps and lumps and poky bits sticking through the paper which made it really exciting, just flat.

So you just knew it was a box of Edinburgh rock or a pair of gloves, or a jigsaw puzzle, or worse still, a book. I mean, whoever sent anyone a book for Christmas? You'd have to read it before you could write the Thank You Letter and you never read a book at holidays. Only at school. Forced.

There was no fun in books or gloves or Edinburgh rock, even though the rock was quite nice, especially the cinnamon bits, but sweets aren't very interesting even in tartan boxes with pictures of Prince's Street on the back. Boring. And gloves. Whoever wants gloves when you've got your own anyway?

So we just knew by the *flatness* what we were in for and left them to the last to open, but we still had to write Thank Yous. Lally kept all the labels and wrote on them saying who they were from and what they had been, because things did get into a bit of a mess on Christmas morning round the tree. So she wrote 'Rock' or 'Book (*Kidnapped*)' or 'Gloves' or 'Long, knitted stockings' to help out at the thanking time.

Long, knitted stockings. Honestly . . .

But some people sent marvellous presents, like another borrowed aunt. She was French, and a famous actress, and we called her Aunt Yvonne and she sent the best presents ever. All bumps and knobs and poky things sticking about. And huge. Once I got a sort of hobby horse with a head and a real grey and white speckly mane, and once a butcher's shop with a butcher, sides of meat, sausages in long pink rows. All in plaster of course, but it was a lovely present. And she always remembered Lally as well and sent her soap, which was very interesting because each piece had a picture of a different dog or a horse on it, and they never wore off, even when the soap got to a little thin sliver of a thing. It was called RSPCA soap, because that's what it had on the box, which made it sound pretty important, and our mother said that Aunt Yvonne had probably bought it at one of the charity bazaars she always had to open, but it was a very kind thought anyway. And Lally said she had enough soap to open a laundry. But she was quite pleased, you could tell.

We always had Christmas together, either at the London house, which was all right but not quite such fun, or the cottage, which was the very best. But once, on a dreadful occasion, we had to go and have it with some real kith and kin that my father had found who belonged to him. It was a bit of a shock, I can tell you. They were what he called his Second Cousins Twice Removed or something. But we still had to go. And even if it sounded quite interesting it wasn't. It was dreadful.

Aunt — well, we had to call her Aunt of course, because even if she was Twice Removed and we didn't like her all that much at first sight she was 'blood' or something — anyway, Aunt Phyllis was terrible. I mean she was quite nice but just didn't understand children, our mother said. And she was married to a man called Digby, who was just as bad but worse really, because he never spoke to us at all except to say 'Herrumph' or 'Now, I'm quite sure you'd like to go for a splendid health-giving walk over our common. Lots of fascinating things to see, you know.' We didn't want to go at all because it was freezing outside, and there wasn't anything to see except awful old dead heather and big, gloomy pine trees. They lived in a most

peculiar house. Our mother said they designed it themselves and it was very modern and advanced. It was
jolly uncomfortable: huge glass windows and no fireplace and all the chairs were made of shiny metal, and
even the dining-table was made of thick glass and silvery
iron stuff.

I ask you . . .

And they didn't even have a Christmas tree because
Uncle (we had to call *him* Uncle too) Digby had asthma
or something, and Aunt Phyllis said they were very dangerous and shed their needles everywhere and made a mess,
and in any case it was all nonsense because it was invented
by the Hun. Our mother said that was her name for the
Germans.

So we just had our presents, which our parents had
brought with them in the car, up in our bedroom. That
was pretty horrible too because it had bunks like on a ship,
and my sister had the lower one and I had to climb an
iron ladder to get into mine, and she was under me and
was terrified all night that I would want to do a pee and
wouldn't bother to go: and then where would she be?

I did see what she meant, but I didn't go, so that was all
right.

There were no flowers anywhere in the house, just
prickly cactus things in big china bowls or square pots,
and a ghastly shiny lady made of brass with her arms
round a sort of clock, sitting on a tiger or something. And
they had a fearful dog, an Alsatian called Hamilcar which
had to wear felt bootees on its feet in the house because it
might scratch Aunt Phyllis's parquet floors. Which were
dreadfully cold and you skidded on.

They didn't eat meat, another bad mark, so my sister and I had a titchy little chicken that she especially cooked for us, which was kind, I suppose, except it was quite cold and was all bloody inside the legs. But there were about fifty different sorts of vegetables like swedes and parsnips and things, and loaves of bread, dark brown, with bits of corn sticking in them. It was all pretty dreadful. After dinner Uncle Digby started to play his gramophone, but not Christmas things like Elsie and Doris Waters or Stanley Holloway, but dreadful serious music which you had to listen to. At least, he did, lying back in his iron chair with leather sides, and his eyes closed, and Aunt Phyllis sitting on a pouf working away at something she said was a rug for the fireplace. Only there wasn't one. I mean, it was just all wonky.

And then Uncle Digby looked at his pocket watch and said, 'Isn't it about time that our young guests were on their way to slumber-land? Too much excitement in one day is not a good thing, is it?'

Too much excitement!

Thank goodness we went home quite early the next day and our father said never again because he'd only been given two measly watered whiskies before dinner, two glasses of thin Australian wine with, and nothing after but a mug of cocoa. And our mother said it wasn't her fault, because they were his relations, and perhaps the next time he was intent on discovering his family he'd have a thought for his own, and if he ever did it again it would be over her dead body. Which worried us a bit because she looked pretty furious – you could see in the car mirror – and we felt a bit uneasy about the dead body part, but she said she didn't mean it quite like that. We asked her. And she explained. Sort of. So that was the Ghastly Farnham Christmas, and we never forgot it ever.

And when we saw Lally again the day after Boxing Day she was all smiling and cheerful and didn't even say that she had missed us, but that they'd had a lovely time at Walnut Cottage, Twickenham, with her father and mother, and they'd had a goose and mince pies, a whole bottle of tonic wine, and Brother Harold had played 'Come, all ye faithful!' on his clarinet, which was Mrs Jane's very favourite.

So that was all right.

We were all in the morning room making paper chains, and Lally was busy mixing a bowl of flour and water paste for us, when there was a terrific crash and we heard our mother calling out, 'Oh! Oh! Oh!' When we rushed into the hall, there she was, sitting all twisty, halfway down the stairs with her hat still on and a white face. Her lips were very red.

Lally called for our father, who was hurrying from his study, and we were sent off to 'keep out of the way', but before we went back to the morning room our mother said she was all right, to us, and not to be worried. But I heard her say to our father, 'Get Henderson, darling,' so I knew she wasn't that all right, because Henderson was our lady doctor. And she also said she was afraid that she would 'lose it', which I didn't understand but thought that perhaps 'it' was her shoe which was lying at the bottom of the stairs, with no heel. So I said, 'Here it is, you haven't lost it really. It's

broken though,' and Lally said be off this minute, and so
we were.

Of course, it wasn't a very nice feeling in the morning
room and the paper chains seemed a bit silly somehow.
There was a lot of coming and going, and then Dr Henderson arrived in her man's suit and tie with her bag, and
hurried up the stairs. And we just sort of mucked about
really, making a few, but not really caring.

'Is she going to die?' said my sister suddenly, and frightened me.

'No. Of course she isn't. She just tripped. I expect she
was in a hurry to go out.'

'I mean it would be so terrible if she died, and especially
at Christmas.'

'Well, she won't. So don't go on moaning.'

'I wasn't moaning. Just saying. That's different.'

And then Lally came in, and she'd changed her overall
and was in a starchy fresh white one, and she went into
the kitchen and put on the kettle, and banged about a bit
and asked us if we were behaving ourselves. Which we
were.

'Is our mother all right now?' I said.

"Course she is. She's as fit as can be, don't you fret.
Mind you,' said Lally, pouring boiling water into the
teapot, 'mind you, I wouldn't swap sit-upons with her.
She'll be black and blue for a fortnight. Those silly heels
she will wear! I've told her and told her. And she's forever
in a hurry.' She took a tray of tea and went into the hall.
'You can come up and see her . . . soon as maybe. She's
had a nasty fall, and she doesn't want a whole tribe of
children traipsing about her bedroom, you see if I'm right.'

She started up the stairs and then turned and looked down at us.

'There's no need for you two to stand there like a couple of empty bottles. She'll be perfectly all right and we're all going down to the cottage for Christmas as arranged. See?'

'All of us?' I said.

'All of us,' she said, going on up slowly and taking care not to spill the little milk jug. 'And don't forget tomorrow! Euston Station quick sharp to meet Cousin Flora. It never rains,' she said going on up as if we couldn't hear her, only we could, 'but it pours!'

Our Cousin Flora was really not bad. Even though she did come from Scotland and was quite difficult to understand when she spoke. Anyway, she was kith and kin, and real not invented. I liked her almost as much as my sister's best friend at the convent, who was Giovanna Govoni and Italian but very easy to understand because she spoke English exactly like us. But Flora was Scots. So that made a difference. Our mother had asked her to come and have Christmas with us all because she didn't have a mother, who had died when she was only a baby. All she had was a brother who was a bit grumpy, and a father who was very frightening and strict, wore rimless glasses and hurt your hand when he shook it and always called me 'young feller'. So it seemed quite a kind thing to do to invite her to stay with us.

A bit later on, just before we went to bed, we were allowed to go and see our mother in her room, which was all shadowy and very nice looking, only she seemed a bit miserable and hadn't got any make-up on, which looked sad too. But she said she was really quite all right, and that she would just have to stay in bed for a few days so we'd have to take over all her responsibilities and look after Cousin Flora and make her feel doubly at home. So we promised we would, and was it all right about going to the cottage for Christmas, and she said yes it was and that we'd go down with Lally on the Green-Line bus, which was terrifically exciting, and she and our father would drive down later on in time for Christmas Eve anyway. Then she seemed a bit weary, and kissed us, and said to be good and help Lally and above all make Cousin Flora feel that she was really and truly wanted.

'How can we do that?' said my sister. 'Make her feel we really want her?'

'I don't know. Tell her, I suppose,' I said.

'But then she might think that if we kept on telling her we did, that we didn't, mightn't she?'

'Well . . . you could give her something of yours that you really liked. I mean that would prove it.'

'What sort of thing?'

'Well . . . that doll of yours, Annabel Lee with the long legs. That.'

My sister gave a terrible screech. 'I love Miss Annabel Lee! She's my very favourite, Aunt Freda gave her to me! I couldn't.'

'It would show Flora that you wanted to make her welcome.'

'But how would she know it was my very favourite thing?'

'You'd say it was. She'd know.'

'And what would you give her then? You'd have to give her something too, *your* most favourite thing.'

'I'm a boy. She wouldn't like my things. Girls don't, you know that. You don't.'

'Well . . . I quite like your Jesus and his Mother. Everyone likes them. You give her them, why not?'

'But they're sacred! I couldn't give them away!'

'Give her your Jesus and Mary, and just see how happy she'll be. That'll make her feel very welcome and wanted. And holy too.'

It gave me a bit of a fright when she said that, so I just finished my Ovaltine and didn't say anything.

'A silence?' said Lally, coming into the morning room where we were having our supper. 'Something's up, out with it. What are you two up to?' She had two fat rubber hot water bottles in her arms, but I knew they were not for us. They were to air Flora's bed. She was sharing my sister's room, which used to be our nursery until I was given my own room because Lally said I was growing up and it wasn't suitable. That's why I had to have my bath separately too, which wasn't as much fun at all, but quite decent really.

'I was just telling him that if he wanted to make Flora feel really happy, and that we were longing for her to come and stay with us, he ought to give her his Jesus and Mary off his silly old altar,' said my sister and slid out of her chair pretty quickly so I couldn't hit her.

'Well, there's a thing!' said Lally in pretend surprise. 'And what, pray, do you think your cousin will want his Jesus and Mary for I'd very much like to know? I'm not sure if they really go in for that sort of thing in Scotland.

Come on now, off to bed, I've got a lot before me one
way and another.'

'Anyway,' said my sister, 'she probably wouldn't because
he's made Jesus all muddly. He painted him with a black
beard and fair hair – that's silly. And he's given Mary
terrible pink cheeks and feet, she looks awful –'

'You just shut up! And M.Y.O.B.,' I said, because I was
suddenly feeling pretty cross and a bit fed up with this Flora.

'Now then!' said Lally, hitting me on the head with one
of the hot water bottles which was a bit hot. 'No more of
that or I'll have that Mr Hitler up to see you off, the pair
of you. All you have to give your cousin is good manners
and a nice smile and that'll do.'

'I don't think I'll give her anything at all,' I said. 'Well,
not at first, not until we know if she's brought us anything
for Christmas.'

'What a horrible-minded child!' said Lally, and started
clearing up our supper tray. 'Be off with you, I shan't tell
you again.'

'If she does bring us a present,' said my sister, tying her
dressing-gown cord tightly round her waist, 'bet it'll be
flat. They always are from Scotland. Flat.'

'This minute, Maddemoselle, if you please!' said Lally
crossly and dropped one of the Ovaltine beakers, and it broke.

'Oh, bless my sister's cats!' she cried. 'Now see what
you've made me do! I'm at the end of my patience. Off!
Hop skip it upstairs, and not a sound when you pass your
mother's door or you'll wish you'd been born next year!'

Flora had fair hair, quite short, in a fringe, and laughed a
lot. She wore a kilt on best occasions, with a huge great

safety pin stuck in it and a hairy purse on a chain round
her waist called a sporran. But all she had in it, that I ever
saw, was one little glass black cat for luck and three pennies. When we met her at Euston Station, she was wearing
her ordinary school clothes, so she was just like anybody
else. She just looked a bit peculiar in her best, in the kilt
and the sporran and all her frills, if you weren't used to it
. . . and quite a lot of people in the streets weren't and
once a man called out something rude about bagpipes and
she stuck out her tongue. Which was pretty terrible, but
no one said anything. I mean Lally didn't, because she said
she'd been 'insulted'.

Her rather grumpy brother Alec wore a kilt too. We
saw him in it once when he came to stay with us on his
own. He was a bit older than me, and bigger, and we all
had to go to a terrible children's party in fancy dress
where you had to walk hand in hand, if you were two, or
just alone, in a long wobbly line with a band playing
something potty like 'In a Persian Market', and people
gave you marks for the Most Original Fancy Dress, or the
Most Beautiful or something. It was really awful, I can tell
you. Except to our mother, who simply loved it. I think
that the children's parties at the Lodge were her very
favourite thing. I suppose it was because she had once been
an actress, so she could do a bit of showing off because she
made all our own clothes, and designed them herself,
although Lally said she didn't really know a needle from a
bodkin.

Anyway, that time my sister went covered in bunches
of glass grapes wearing a silly pair of string sandals with a
wreath of vine leaves in her hair which prickled like any-

thing. And she was called 'Bacchanti'. And I had to wear a really quite stinky old fur rug tied round me, and the same kind of sandals, and carry a wooden sort of flute thing which was all pretend really, because our father had made it for me with some wire and a broken bit of fishing rod. I mean, it didn't play or anything, it was just for carrying. And I was told I was a Greek shepherd. It was really terrible. And what made it more sickening than anything was that boring Alec just went in his 'best', I mean his kilt and a velvet jacket and a lot of silver buttons. I was pretty fed up because I smelt so rotten. It was quite an old goat-skin thing my mother had found in our father's studio, and it tickled as well, and I was all tied up in it like a parcel, with bits of thick string. And what made it worst of all was that Alec won. Of course.

I mean, honestly! Getting first prize for wearing your *own* clothes!

But it was a bit funny later because they made him have a ride on the pantomime horse, all round the ballroom. It wasn't really a horse, you know, it was only two men in a sort of spotted suit with a huge hee-haw head and a funny tail, and Alec went red in the face, and wouldn't. Everyone laughed and pulled him, so he had to get on, but you could see he was pretty fed up and had to hold on terrifically tightly because actually what they were trying to do was to bump him off and make him look silly. And then they did a stupid sort of pantomime dance all round the room, and everyone cheered and clapped, and Alec was looking sort of white and pretty upset because he was afraid that with all the bumping he was getting his kilt would blow up and everyone would see his tartan knickers.

It did. And everyone roared with laughter and waved their arms in the air, which only goes to show that grown-ups can be pretty silly sometimes. I felt quite sorry for him, but I was very glad then that I didn't win a prize in my goatskin, and I told our mother that if we had to do it again next year I would go as something quite good and exciting. Like a deep-sea diver.

Chapter 4

The night before we had to catch the Green Line bus from Victoria, the packing began. It was all right for Flora because she was already packed on account of coming from Scotland to visit us, so she had an advantage. But she sort of hung about watching us pack our things, which was a bit irritating because she would keep on asking why we were taking this and that just for a short journey and a short holiday. So I just told her to M.Y.O.B., which she didn't understand until I said, quite loudly so that she did, 'It means Mind Your Own Business. That's what it means!' and she just shrugged and told me not to be so huffy and I nearly hit her with my box of Venus pencils, but they might have got broken so I didn't.

My sister was putting all her treasures, as she called them, into a little attaché case which our father had given her because the handle had broken. She was a bit silly about calling them 'treasures' because they weren't at all valuable and treasure is. Her things were potty, really a set of cigarette cards of 'Famous Cricketers' for example, and a mussel shell from the Cuckmere, and a whole set of Tiny Tots transfers which she had never even used because she said it would spoil them if you stuck them on things. Honestly! It was a bit annoying because I had used mine all up, and she had 'Christian Names' (and their meaning), 'Pantomimes' and 'Methods of Transport', and she kept them in a book, but what good they were to her I never could understand because they were all back-to-front. Girls are a bit soppy sometimes.

I just had a rather decent penknife with *R.M.S. Majestic* painted on it, and my Venus pencils in a cardboard box, quite long, and smelling of cedarwood, a drawing-block I quite liked because it fitted in a jacket pocket and you could do 'quick sketches' in the field, our father said – he used one in his war and he was doing serious drawings of fighting in the Great War for *The Times*, so he should know what he was talking about – and then, of course, top of the list, there were Sat and Sun, my mice, in their neat wooden cage. It had a glass front you could slide out for cleaning, and a wheel, for running, and a little house in the corner where they made their nest. Flora wanted to know why they were called Sat and Sun and I said they just were, and everyone in the family knew them just as the Weekend. She looked very thoughtful. But it shut her up.

They had to live in their cage in the morning room. I wasn't allowed to have them in my bedroom, worse luck, on account of the smell, which I didn't mind but Lally and our mother did. When Lally saw me putting newspaper all over the dining-table, as I had to every time I cleaned them out, she made a heavy sighing sound and dumped a big pile of folded shirts and things on the wickerwork chair by the Ideal boiler.

'For mercy's sake! What will we do supposing the conductor on the bus says no mice allowed? What then, I would like to know? How are you going to get yourself, and the Weekend, all the way back to Hampstead from Victoria with not a penny in your pocket? Tell me that or forever hold your tongue.'

Well, I knew she didn't mean it because she knew the

Weekend was coming with us and I was going to have to hold it on my knee all the way to Seaford, but she was just being pretend angry and she knew very well that the conductor would be jolly interested in Sat and Sun because one was black and one was white. And if he wasn't I'd make him, by telling him that he could have one of their babies if he liked, a black or a white, and Lally said, when I told her, that she hoped the Miracle wouldn't happen on the bus or at the rest-stop because *she* would have nothing to do with a litter of pink white mice all blind and naked. It was a bit upsetting really, and I was worried that she might be right, and then what would I do? No one to help, and it might be a terrible shock to them. So I didn't say anything, but just found the Jeyes Fluid and a brush and got ready to do a bit of cleaning before the long journey.

It was pretty exciting sitting in the Green Line bus – we weren't usually allowed to do this on account of germs and things. But Lally said that in the very cold weather, like December, and with a sharp frost, it would not be so dangerous, the germs would be killed off. So we felt quite safe as we left Victoria Coach Station and went across the river heading to Sussex.

I had to sit beside Flora, which was all right because she didn't seem to mind about the Weekend on my knees, and Lally and my sister sat together behind us with the attaché case and a little wicker basket in which we knew were the sandwiches, Thermos flask and some fruit which we would have when we got to Felbridge in an hour's time. About.

It was quite a decent omnibus. It had an orange and brown ziggy-zaggy carpet, so as not to show the dirt,

Lally said, and curtains at the windows to keep out the sun if you had to. The people travelling with us seemed to me to be quite all right. I mean, what you could see of them, because they were all wrapped up with woollen scarves, travelling-rugs and tweedy coats. Some of the men wore caps which they didn't take off even when the omnibus had started on the journey. Quite rude really. But when I looked round at them all, sitting in their seats like brown paper parcels, they all smiled back and nodded at me, which made it all feel rather comfortable. After all, we were all going on a journey, and it's better to have pleasant people with you on that sort of a thing than grumpy ones. What was especially good was that no one seemed to be interested in the Weekend. I mean, I didn't show anyone, but no one even looked curious, like most grown-up people do. They were quite busy unwrapping their mufflers and looking for the return half of their tickets, and unbuttoning coats, and that sort of thing. So I just said nothing, only smiled, in case they might decide that there was a funny smell. Or something. You can't ever be sure. Anyway, there wasn't. Just the Jeyes Fluid.

The conductor was very nice indeed too. I mean, he didn't say anything, hardly looked at me really, so he couldn't have seen the cage on my knees, and just asked Lally for the tickets and told her we'd have to change at Lewes.

So that was all right, and when she said that she hoped very much indeed that we could catch our connection from there to Seaford, he said that he hoped we'd get there himself. He hadn't actually got a connection to catch there but he did have a 'connection', if we knew what he

meant (which we didn't), because his sister would be waiting at the bus station for the package he was bringing her
on account of not trusting the Royal Mail at Christmas.

'Oh my word!' said Lally kindly. 'You would be vexed
should we be late, just as we shall be vexed if we don't get
to Seaford. I only hope you are not conveying anything
perishable, like fish or something, that would be very
alarming.'

And he just laughed and said, 'Fish to Seaford is as coals
to Newcastle, upon my word!' and then he said no, he
was taking her some special wool for a rug she was hook-
ing to go beside her bed. She'd run out of orange and
could only get the true colour she needed in Selfridge's.

'Fancy!' said Lally, not much caring really.

'Making a sunset effect,' said the conductor and went
away whistling. So that was quite all right, and he never
so much as glanced at the Weekend on my knees.

In a while we started off. A terrific swerving, clouds of
black smoke, and rows of pale faces staring up as we set
off on the journey.

Outside the bus everything was frosty and grey-coloured
with wispy drifts of misty-fog floating over the hedges
and through the branches of the trees. It looked quite as if
someone was cooking a huge cabbage in a steamer, or else
boiling up all the household sheets in the copper. Outside
looked exactly like our scullery. Only not as warm. There
were dribbles of water running down the windows, and
the inside of the bus felt really quite cold suddenly, which
it would do of course, because we had now left the city
and were out in the countryside. Well, almost countryside.
There were rows of houses with sheds leaning against

them, or old bicycles, or rabbit hutches, and there were
lace curtains at all the windows and pointy gables and
titchy little gardens with sundials in the middle or tin
baths hanging on the walls. And then, quite suddenly,
they began to trail off. The lamp-posts ended, the road
got narrower, and all at once we were out in the real
country. You could see that easily through the dribbles
down the window and the steam bits. I wiped them away
with my sleeve, and outside it was all white, drifting mists,
black trees and, now and again, a miserable horse standing
with bowed head close to the hedges. Sometimes, in a
quite wide field, there would be a herd of cows standing
together, switching their tails, breathing out snorts of
cloud, and then they would all begin to break away and
clomp across the frozen grass because a man was coming
towards them with a horse and cart full of bales of hay. It
was very interesting. If you liked that kind of thing.

Then we got to the rest-stop at Felbridge and that was
almost half the journey over. The café was by the side of
the road with a big car park for the bus. It was surrounded
by sad-looking birch trees and drooping rhododendrons
and dead bracken, and everywhere the grass was spiked
with ice, or frost. When the bus stopped everyone
scrambled off and hurried across the car park to the lavs,
and when we got into the actual café it was much better
and smelled of varnish and wood and HP Sauce and fried
eggs, so that you really felt quite hungry.

It was very warm, and the huge tea urn was hissing
away just like a railway engine at a station, but Lally gave
me a shove and told me not to dawdle, which I wasn't
anyway, and bagged a table and dumped her wicker basket

on the top. She told us all to sit round and make it look full up. Which it was with four of us and the Weekend beside my chair. I was a bit worried that the heat might draw out the smell, but it didn't seem to, and I had covered the whole of the cage in what Lally called 'stout brown paper', so that no one would guess what it had inside. People would think that it was just a plain, ordinary, old brown paper parcel and not get the wind up. You can't tell with grown-ups.

I tore off one corner of the paper before I set it on the floor just to see if everyone was all right inside. And everyone was: I just saw a pink foot and a little sniffling nose and felt very comforted to think that they were having an adventure like us. They had sawdust all over their floor, and a whole folded page of the *Daily Mail* to sop up anything which might have made a stink. They hadn't died of fright or anything, which they easily could have, with all the banging about and bumps and swinging, and then Lally told me to put them down quick sharp or risk a sharp cuff, so I did. No point in getting a good cuffing, as she called it, in front of hundreds of strange people. She could cuff pretty hard when she wanted to.

The sandwiches were all spread out neatly on little paper napkins. Four each: bloater paste, egg and cress, Kraft cheese, and chicken and ham paste. It was quite good really. And when the Thermos came out, and the four cups were unwrapped and set about, and the sugar counted out carefully, one lump each, in a napkin, it all seemed Christmassy already. It really was a winter picnic. I rather liked it. We were never allowed to have tea out of the big hissing urn on account of 'foreign bodies' and chipped cups and 'how-long-do-you-think-it's-been-stewing-I'd-like-to-know?'

So we just had home-made, and it was pretty awful. It always tasted of tin, but our father said it was tannin but didn't explain what that was. Anyway, it was pretty rotten, but hot. We couldn't dawdle really, had to eat quite fast because the rest was only for half an hour and some people hadn't even got their tea from the urn and were eating fat bun-things with white sugar on top. I liked the look of them, and I would have asked if I could have bought one, only Flora began to rustle about in her satchel-thing. It had a strap and hung over her shoulder and had a big ink blot on it, so I knew it was her best for school.

I was pretty interested really because I thought that perhaps she might be fishing about for a piece of Edinburgh rock, and that put me off thinking about the sugar-bun, and then Lally said, very kindly, 'What are you looking for, Flora dear? A hanky?' She was always kind to guests and used her Patient Voice. They were not what she called 'her children', like we were, so she took particular care to be absolutely lovely to them and that way she could be pretty rotten to us because we belonged to her and she was trying to make us into little ladies and gentlemen. Except, I wasn't interested. Which is why she could give you a cuff.

Anyway, Flora was mucking about, tumbling things over in her satchel and beginning to whine. Girls always do, it seems. Her face screwed up like an old glove, all bumps and creases.

'Whatever is it, Flora?' said Lally in her Patient Voice.

'Oh! Oh, dearie me! Dearie-me-today!' wailed Flora. 'I

can't find my wee black cat and it brings me luck and I've had him all my life and if I can't find him, then I'll just die. Here at this very table.'

'That won't do. Won't do at all,' said Lally a bit sharply.

My sister didn't say anything. She just sat quietly chewing her egg and cress and swinging her legs. If she hadn't been so busy chewing her sandwich she would have had a rather nasty smile on her face, but she just chewed, and bits of cress slid down her chin, and she went on chewing away watching wretched Flora.

Suddenly Lally grabbed the satchel and pulled out a terrific clutter of matchboxes, hair slides, a bit of ribbon, half a stick of liquorice, an empty scent bottle and a hair brush full of blond hair. And there, among the bristles and the old bits of Flora's hair, was her black cat.

'Oh!' cried Flora. 'You found him! How *ever* can I thank you, pray?'

'Don't want you falling dead in the middle of the Felbridge rest-café, do we?' She started being brisk with the paper napkins and the cork of the Thermos. 'Now then, quick sharp. We'll be off soon, I reckon.'

Flora was mooning away like anything over her silly glass cat which hadn't even been lost. Anyway, it was only as big as a fingernail, hardly worth bothering about.

'Now all of you eat up. I declare we'll be on our way because the driver and that very polite conductor have put on their caps, and that's the signal for us to be off again. Quick sharp, please!'

Flora stuffed the last piece of chicken and ham into her mouth and showed me the stupid cat.

'Look! He's so pretty. He's got a wee gold collar, see? And green diamond eyes. He's terribly pretty, I think.'

'There are no such things as green diamonds,' I said.

'There are too! He's got them! So there must be. Look how they wink! That's why he's lucky, he knows.'

My sister had finished her sandwich and was swallowing hard, and at the same time pressed her fingertips on all the spilled crumbs on the table top. She was always greedy, and she put them on her lips and licked them in and ate them slowly. 'I got one of those cats once, from a cracker,' she said.

Flora looked at her with hatred. 'Liar!' she said, and Lally almost lifted her hand to give her a good cuff but remembered the guest-bit.

'None of that, please! We'll have good manners here.'

'It was last Christmas, and mine had red diamond eyes. Didn't it Lally? *Red* ones. I remember.'

'Rubies,' I said, and Flora twisted her face to begin whining again, but Lally gave me one of her looks and wrapped everything up in a clean tea-cloth.

'Red or green makes no difference, no difference at all. Both are lucky, and *we* better be lucky and start to move. The driver has just trodden on his cigarette butt, and that's a sure sign. So anyone who wants to be "excused" had better go off and do it now. Be off this instant – it's a long journey ahead.'

Going back to the bus was quite difficult. It was icy, and our feet crunched over the tarmac and I held on to the Weekend very tightly for fear of them falling or something. It was quite worrying trying not to bang them against my knees, and Lally said she was worried about

the other end, when we got to the cottage, because the
way up from the road was a narrow chalk path, and it
would likely be iced over in the dark of the trees. You
couldn't even ride a bike up it in the summer, it was so
steep, so how will we manage with all the luggage and
that dratted cage, she'd like to know? I knew she was
worried because she said 'dratted'. In front of a guest.

When we got into the bus and settled ourselves down,
and she had counted the luggage on the rack, I said that
perhaps Mrs Daukes, who lived in the cottage at the foot
of the path, might give us a hand, or her husband, Mr
Daukes.

Lally snorted, and resettled her hat with the ivy leaves.
'Mrs Daukes hasn't been known to give anyone a helping
hand, nor anything else for that matter. A sly woman,
Mrs Daukes. *He'll* be down at the Magpie getting ready
for Christmas. We'll be lucky if she's even aired the house.
Though I wrote most particular and advised her of our
impending arrival. But I wonder?'

Lally didn't like Mrs Daukes because once last summer,
when our parents came down to the cottage, without warning, they had discovered her sitting in her garden wearing
a pair of our mother's ankle-strap shoes from Paris.
There was a terrible fuss, so now there was no knowing
what we'd find. She could have set fire to the place. Or
put the pink carbolic powder we used in the privy down
the well. You couldn't really trust her after that shoe
business.

At Lewes it was already almost dark. There were lights
in some of the shops up the hill, the lamp-posts were on,
and by the time we had clambered off, said our thanks to

the driver and the conductor and got on to the Seaford bus which would take us on over High-And-Over and down to Alfriston, it was really quite dark, and we only caught the bus because Lally waved her umbrella and shouted very loudly. And then we were safely on board.

After we moved out of Seaford there were only four other people left on the bus except for us: Ivy Bottle, who lived down Sloop Lane and was pretty boring, my mother said; Mr and Mrs Wooler, who were quite old and friends of the vicar's sisters, Misses Ethel and Maude who ran the little shop down by the Flats, the water-meadows which got flooded in winter at high tide; and another person we did not know. Everyone we did know called out and said how nice it was to see us all again and were we down for Christmas, and how was our mother and so on. It was very friendly and welcoming and I nearly told them about the Weekend, but a poke in the side from Lally made me change my mind.

Then the headlights of the bus swept across the old flint walls and the bobbly windows of Baker's the confectioner's and the bulging panes of glass in the double windows of Wilde's the grocer's, and then, like a skinny finger wearing a thimble, right in the middle of the square, there was the Market Cross and we knew we were safely home at last.

It seemed like the middle of the night, it was so dark, and we had to unload all our packages and cases, and call out to Ivy Bottle and the Woolers. Then we had to go and stand under the chestnut tree outside Waterloo Cottages and wait for Ted Deakin to arrive with his lorry, which he did pretty soon – well, just before we all wanted to be excused. I mean, just in time. His lorry arrived and made a half-turn under the tree, and he called out to us that we'd be home in a jiffy and jumped down to help load the baggage.

Flora was a bit worried because she saw *Deakin and Son, Undertakers and General Removers* printed on the side of the lorry, but I told her that it was perfectly all right. This was Deakin's lorry, not the hearse. She felt a bit better when she was told to go and sit in the front cabin part with Lally while my sister and I had to squat among our baggage in the back.

It was jolly cold, I can tell you. But what was more frightening in the dark was a huge old sideboard which kept sliding about with its doors flapping open and shut every time we turned a corner.

'If it falls on us we'll be squashed flat,' said my sister. 'And no one will hear if we scream for help. I think it's a vile thing to do, all that way from London.'

That rather worried me: supposing it squashed the Week-end as well?

'What does he want a terrible old thing like that for in his lorry?' said my sister, pushing against it with one foot. 'I can't hold it back. You push too.'

So we sat there pushing the sideboard while its doors slammed and opened like clapping hands. We couldn't really see it because it was so dark, just a shape, but we knew what it was because we had seen it lit up by the lamps in Wood's the butcher's, down in the square, where they were just shutting up the shop and scrubbing down the counter and the chopping-block, and Mrs Wood, who was quite fat and sat in the cash desk, was sweeping out the sawdust. That's how we saw the sideboard, pulling our suitcases and bags on board. And then suddenly we felt a turn to the left, very swervy, and the sideboard slid across the lorry and we crouched in the corners and then the worst thing happened. We began to climb the hill up to the cottage and the sideboard rattled very fast down to the end of the lorry and crashed against the tailboard, where it stuck with all our bags clustered round it like piglets at a sow.

It was quite funny in a kind of way, because I knew we were going up all the way, so it wouldn't slither back and flatten us. And there was the wonderful smell of dung from the sties at Piggy Corner, and I called out to my sister that we were nearly home and she called back that she would have to be excused in a minute, she was 'terrified' by the sliding sideboard and had wanted to 'go' ever since we left the Market Cross.

But then we stopped and I heard Lally getting down and calling to Flora and heard her hurrying round to the back of the lorry with her dancing torch.

'Oh my Lord!' she cried. 'Mr Deakin, I declare you've killed the children! Or else where are they?' Then we clambered out into the road.

'Good riddance!' he shouted and drove off up the hill towards Milton Street, whistling like anything, leaving us standing at the path up to the cottage with all the luggage. There was a lamp glimmering in Mrs Daukes's cottage, and pretty soon she came out and we all shook hands and started up the path with bags and cases, everyone carrying something.

'I laid the fire,' said Mrs Daukes. 'All you 'ave to do is touch 'im with a match. 'Ave a nice glow in no time. I got some nice dry kindling, and there's half that old apple as fell in October last.'

Lally used her Extra-Polite voice, which could be a bit dangerous sometimes. 'That's a kindness, Mrs Daukes, to be sure,' she said.

'Well, I 'eard the door a'slammin'. That'll be the Rectory people, I'll be bound, I said to Mr Daukes, sat there in his chair. And so t'were! Out I come, and there you was.'

She was swinging her hurricane lamp about like a censer in St Catherine's, which was all right for her because she was leading, and in the front, but *I* couldn't see anything. I was humping the Weekend in one hand and Flora's boring bag of presents in the other. Jolly heavy they were, but I almost felt cheerful because whatever they were this time, they couldn't be just books or boxes of Edinburgh rock. They were round. But there were just little slits of light from Mrs Daukes's lamp and spots from Lally's torch which waggled about on the dead grasses along the path. Flora moaned about how much further it would be, and my sister started whining about wanting to 'go' pretty quickly, which reminded me that I wouldn't mind myself. Then I saw the bobbly stalk of some old Brussels sprouts and I knew we were going through the vegetable garden and that meant the front door was near.

'Mr Daukes poorly, then, is he? I mean, him in a chair and not in the pub?' said Lally, stepping over a broken cloche.

''E took a nasty fall last week. *Very* nasty it was. Tripped on them cobbles down by the Cross. Caught 'im on the head something cruel. All bloody he were, and Dr Wilmott had to give him a couple of stitches.'

We had reached the front door, and Lally was fumbling in her bag for the key and her torch was sticking up in the air like a searchlight. So that wasn't much good.

'I'm sure he'll be right as rain shortly,' said Lally. 'Thank you for the hurricane lamp, it'll see you home again.'

Mrs Daukes bobbed about and then we were all in the lean-to and the lovely smell of winter onions and paraffin was everywhere, and I knew we were back at the cottage.

'If you ask me,' said Lally, taking off her gloves in the darkness and starting to light one of the lamps, 'Dr Wilmott could have obliged us all by putting a couple of stitches in his lips. Stop him imbibing. Now, look sharp, Mr Head-in-the-air, light up some candles.'

They were all set in a neat row, just as we had left them last time, ranged along the work-bench, little white enamel candlesticks with red and blue bands round them. I knew my one quickly, because it had a bad dent on it where I had dropped it years ago, and the white all came off and there was a scabby place like a map of Australia.

Flora said that she thought it was very dark and witchy, and had I got her presents, and my sister started whining away, and Lally said, 'Outside, my girl, if you can't wait, or fetch yourself your potty. Take a candle with you.'

And then she shrugged off her best check coat, and started to take off the halo-hat with the ivy leaves. And that was the sign that we had really arrived.

It was very nice indeed sitting round the big table in the kitchen in the lamplight. The fire was crackling in the range, there were two kettles hissing quietly on the Primus stoves on the top of the copper getting ready for the

the lean-to.

washing up part, and we had all had a 'delicate sufficiency', as Lally said, of a Melton Mowbray pie, cut in four chunks, pork and beans, tinned (which was not allowed by our father, who said we'd get ptomaine poisoning from things in tins). Lally had hidden this one away in her bag because it was an emergency.

The only rotten part was that she gave wretched Flora the lovely bit of pork because she was the Guest. Well, you might have guessed that. Guests were always favourite. There were some apples from last year, for afters, and Lally had a big piece of cheese with some pickled onions which were on the shelf in the lean-to.

'At least we didn't have Mrs Daukes pinching the pickled onions, and judging by her roving eye and wandering hand we very likely might have, and that would not have pleased your father. Loves his pickled onion, he does. I put up ten pounds in September. They won't last to Christmas, not with him!'

'He'll have my presents,' said Flora.

'He simply *hates* Edinburgh rock. All he really likes is wine gums or Rowntrees Fruit Gums. The clear ones,' said my sister, nodding her head.

'Who does?' asked Flora, looking worriedly at me because I had had to lumber her wretched 'presents' all the way from Ted Deakin's cart.

'Well, our father. He's particular, he doesn't like sweet things.'

Lally got up and began stacking the plates, scraping off the bits into a bowl by the pickled onions. 'Now, come along! We've all had a tiring day, the bricks are in the oven, and all your beds are made down. And they don't lie, my children, their father can't abide sweet things.' She started off towards the sink, making head signs to us to follow. So I scraped my plate, and stacked my sister's, and reached for Flora's, who hit my hand and said she'd take it. And Lally said, '*No*. No sweet things ... except of course your actual Rowntrees Fruit Gums, clear, in a tube, and your actual Maynards Wine Gums. *Those* he likes. For all the port wine is green and the sherry is black. But those he likes ... and hand me over a kettle quick as may be.'

Flora offered her dirty plate. 'It's nothing sweet ... they are two lovely haggis. And a Black-Man's-Ear!' she said.

Lally had soap suds up to her elbow. 'Black-Man's what?' she said, and you could see she was alarmed.

So I said, because I already knew, from being up in that dreadful country, that she really meant a black pudding. So that was all right, and our father loved haggis, although Lally said it had taken her a little time to 'get used to them'. But she only had them once a year, and the getting-used-to was a bit of a shock every time. 'As long as you don't dwell on what they are made of, you'll come to no harm,' she said. 'There is a very big difference between the words "composed" and "de-composed", and that'll do for the moment. Savoury, that's what your father says, and savoury they certainly are.'

When we finished the washing-up, and put the plates and things back on the dresser, had a game of Snakes and Ladders, and two of Happy Families, we had to take the bricks out of the oven in the range, wrap them in bits of an old flannel shirt which had belonged to her father, Mr Jane, and put them in our beds. My sister and I were in our room, the first one, Flora had the second one, and

Lally was right at the end, in hers. But we all had doors between each other, so when Lally called out 'Goodnight, be good!' we all heard her. But this time she called out and said to remember that in two days' time it would be Christmas Eve, and that our father and mother would be with us, and they'd bring Minnehaha our cat, and a goose and presents, and that we had to be quiet with our mother because she had had a 'nasty time of it', and so we were to be respectful and kind. And did we hear all that? And we all yelled through from our rooms, 'Yes!', so that was all right.

My sister huffled and fuffled about in her bed across the room.

'Whatever are you doing?'

'Trying to find the comfortable part. I've forgotten since last time. Do you like Flora? I mean really *like* her?'

'Not much. But whisper. She's next door, and it's open.'

'What is?'

'The door.'

She huffled and fuffled a bit more. Then she said suddenly, 'Did you show her her potty? With the pheasant on the bottom?'

'Yes. She looked worried. I think she'll save it all up until morning.'

'Save what all up?'

'Widdle.'

'Oh. I see. These Scots people. Really. But it's good about no books or socks and just haggis. Isn't it?'

'And our father and mother and Minnehaha . . . I am a bit worried about Sat and Sun. They drive him wild. He can smell them.'

'Well, put them on a shelf in the lean-to.'

'It's cold there.'

'I think it's very nice being back again. Don't you . . .?'

But her voice was getting a bit faded, so I just agreed. But I did feel it was very nice, the candlestick with Australia on the chair beside my bed, the Weekend safe, fed and watered, on the shelf by the stairs, Flora asleep in the next room, and being with Lally. Because, apart from our parents, Lally was the best person in all the world, even if she did cuff me a bit and make me cart the water up in buckets and bury the Bindie Bucket and everything. She made it all feel safe, and loving.

Just through the wall I could hear her snoring. It was very nice indeed.

Chapter 5

I was just lying there: it was very warm and safe-feeling. I knew it was still dark because there was no ragged line of light round the curtains and I could hear Flora snoring, or moaning, in her bed. My sister was probably curled up with her head under the quilt. She always slept like that, only this time I couldn't see her because it was dark. But if I turned my head and looked through Flora's room I could see the orange glimmer round Lally's bedroom door, and that was her getting up. So, worse luck, as soon as she'd got on her pinafore, tidied up her hair and shaken her alarm clock (she always did this to see if it was still working even though she could hear it ticking, but it was just something she did anyway, to be quite certain), I knew the door would creak open and she'd come through the rooms and tell us to start waking up, quick sharp, and that another day was starting and there was this or that to do if we wanted any breakfast. I knew it by heart, I suppose.

'Time to wake up! Lots to do before breakfast!' she said. (You see?) And then she saw I was awake 'There's a surprise for you all outside . . . better get your skates on before it goes.' She was holding her candle high so that shadows danced across the bumpy plaster walls and made the beams black and wavery. She had her indoor shoes in her other hand, so as not to wake us up, except that she had already woken us.

'What is it?' I said and sat up, and felt the cold slither right down my back.

'Been a fall of snow overnight. Still as still ... but it won't lie. Best put on your woolly stockings from the top drawer. It's a very cold morning.' And then she opened the door to the stairs and went rustling down while I reached for the box of Swan Vestas by the candlestick.

When we all got down to the kitchen, and after I'd looked to see if all was well with the Weekend (which it was), the light was goldeny brown from the paraffin lamp and the candle, and the range was crackling and Lally was pumping up the Primus ... the other one had a singing kettle on it – well, not exactly singing, but sighing really. It was still dark outside, but if you pressed hard against the cold glass, and shaded your face against the lamplight with your hands, you could see, as clear as clear, that everything outside was white.

'It'll be light in a few minutes, near eight o'clock, and as soon as it is, and as soon as you've had a good hot drink, taken your Virol, got on your Wellingtons, then it's off with you all to do a bit of wooding for the kindling pile while I get the toast and porridge ready. And I want no arguments!' She looked very serious, one hand on hip, bread knife in the other. I mean, it was sticking up! You couldn't argue with her.

'What's for breakfast?' I said, pouring milk from the milk-can into a jug.

'Tea, toast and six eggs! And out of my way, I've a busy day today.' She wagged the knife at me, 'Toot de sweet, now!'

My sister came clumping down the stairs doing up her snake-belt. It was her most favourite thing, and she'd pinched it from me, but I had a second, so it didn't worry me really. But she wore it even with her good flannel skirt from school. Not just her shorts, like she did in summer. 'You said it was snowing!' she grumbled. 'That's what you said,' and she began to pull up her school socks which were woollen and awful-looking things. Wrinkled grey worms.

'It *was* snowing! I said there had been a light fall, if I'm right – and no one try to correct me. It's stopped now, and you'll come to no harm and I reckon you won't see a polar bear, no more a penguin, where you are going. And please set the sugar on the table. Flora! Flora! Come along now, do. Breakfast is about to begin. Flora! Do I have to bang a gong?'

'She wouldn't know what a gong was,' I said. 'And the wood will be all snowy, all the kindling and everything.'

'So what's the use?' said my sister huffing about looking for the Tate and Lyle on the dresser.

'The use is that I need the kindling, so shake the snow off – don't dare bring it into the house and make all the rest sodden!'

'But there is masses of kindling, we got piles yesterday!'

'And you'll get piles today! Or else my name is not Ellen Jane . . .'

My sister looked at me across the table and made a twisty face, and we both began to snort a bit, and Lally suddenly got a bit red in the face, the way she did when she thought we were being rotten behind her back but she didn't know. Like the Bindie Bucket business.

'What's all the sniggering in aid of, pray? That range uses the kindling like straw, and there's the sitting-room fire to be lit to air the room for your parents, and I want the copper lit this afternoon . . .' She started to slice up the big cottage loaf for toast. You could see she was being a bit huffy about the sniggering part because she suddenly said, quite crossly, 'Your grammar! Upon my word! What would your father say? "Good Grammar Teached Here Gooder Up The Stairs." That's what. "Is" and "are", remember. And now out of my way.'

But you could see she was fretting, and then Flora came down the stairs looking pretty silly in a raggedy woollen red and yellow tartan hat which she said was her Tam o'Shanter. And it had a stupid pom-pom on the top which wobbled about. She looked really jolly funny, wandering about the kitchen pulling the hat this way and that.

Lally took the kettle off the Primus and poured it into the big brown teapot. 'I want no more private laughter from you two,' she said, 'and no *quibbling*! No quibbling at all. Wooding after your tea and Virol, breakfast *after*. Then you all get washed and do teeth.' And looking at Flora she said, in her Polite-to-Guest voice, 'Flora dear, what are you about? Not in the house dear, not in the house.' And then she set the jar of Virol on a saucer and put three spoons round it, like the spokes in a wheel.

Flora pulled out her chair and sat down. She wasn't a bit afraid of Lally, mostly because Lally was always so terribly sweet to her. When she spoke to her, anyway.

'It's against the cold,' she said firmly. I thought she was very brave. 'My father says that our heads are like yon chimney. All the heat in your body just rises up and goes out of the top of your head. And he was a soldier in the war and he should know.'

'Well . . . quite right. But your head will be nice and

warm in my kitchen, now I've got it all cosy and comfy for you, so I'll be obliged if you'd remove your hat at my table, please. You'll lose nothing through the top of your head except your brains. Off with it, please, Madam Caledonia!'

So Lally won. Well, she nearly always did. So the silly Tam o'Shanter came off and we drank our tea, had the Virol and licked the spoons.

Lally poured herself another cup of tea. 'I'm not washing all that money down the drains! You lick it clean. Cost your parents a lot of money to keep you healthy. Lick now! Quick sharp! It's just like caramel!'

She was being really quite bullying, but it was now light outside, and she was in a hurry. 'I'll need milk today. So when you've done the wooding and washed, and if the snow isn't too thick, I'll thank you to hop skip it down to the dairy and ask Miss Aleford, if she's there, or Len Diplock if he's in the yard, for two pints of fresh –' and then she stopped and said we'd never remember, and so when we came back from the wooding she'd have a list. And to hurry up about it.

The snow wasn't really thick. We left footprints, but it wasn't right up to our knees or anything wonderful like that, or even up to our ankles. It was just white. But everything was very still and early morning. Down at the Court, where we had to go for the milk, there was a waver of thin smoke meandering up in the air, and my sister said that at least *someone* else was up at dawn, and not just us.

Flora stood looking at the whiteness. The sky was grey with little orange specks in it like the back of a plaice. The

Downs were smooth and soft, and you couldn't even see the white horse on High-And-Over because he was covered, and so was the gorse. Everything was smooth and clean like big fat pillows. I almost really liked Flora when she said that the cottage looked like a 'wee ship' in a white sea. But I *knew* it looked like a ship, I just found the 'wee' part boring: it was the way she spoke. And the cottage did look strange up on the very top of Great Meadow with nothing, except the elms round the church, for miles and miles. We started wooding away, but secretly I was a bit worried that perhaps our parents wouldn't be able to get up the road. The O.M. was the best car in the world, but the lane to the cottage was deep in snow. Only I didn't say anything, except to tell Flora not to pick up any old bits of elderberry bush. She was stuffing the wooding-sack full with it, and I had to take it all out and explain to her why not.

'Well! *Why* not? It's as dry as dry. It just snaps –'

'And it smells terrible on the fire. All the house smells if you burn it.'

'Smells of what? What does it smell of?'

My sister looked at me with a squinty smiling face. 'You tell her,' she said.

'No, you. You're the girl.'

'Whatever has *that* got to do with it?'

'Well. You are both girls. It's easier to tell a girl if you are a girl.'

'My feet are cold, thank you kindly,' said Flora. 'So what *do* I gather if I don't gather the easy stuff. Elderberry. And why not? You haven't said.'

'Because,' I said, with my breath drifting out round me

like fog, 'because it smells of bindie. That's why. So don't pick it up.'

Flora looked pinched, but she just shrugged. 'I don't know what you mean. I think you are being horrid and making me feel daft because I'm Scots! Well I am and I don't. Feel silly, I mean. I don't know what your old bindie means so I'll just go on picking it up. So there.'

'It smells like *dog's* bindie,' hissed my sister.

Flora went quite white. She dropped some sticks and looked worried. 'What's bindie for goodness' sake? What's that?'

My sister started to drag the wooding-sack through the snow across the little churchyard where we were looking for the kindling among the ash and the elms. 'It's what dogs do in the street. Not at lamp-posts, that's just widdle. Bindie is much worse. *Much* worse. And that's what elder-berry wood smells of.'

Flora screamed suddenly, her Tam o'Shanter went tilty, and she beat her hands against her coat.

'It's everywhere! I can smell it! It's terrible! My coat is ruined. Oh dearie me —'

'No need to deary-you. It only smells like it in the fire. That's all. I mean, there isn't any bindie actually *on* the twigs . . .'

But she covered her ears up and started to scramble down the path to the gate. 'You *are* awful! Awful! I feel sick. I'll go and tell on you two . . .'

I watched her sliding and stumbling down the hill. But we had work to do.

'Let her go. Good riddance,' said my sister. 'So silly about a little bit of bindie. Goodness. Anyway, she gets in the way. We can do it quicker together because we know what is and what isn't. After we've got the milk, will you come to Baker's with me? There is a dear little matchbox there with a whole fishing-kit inside. It's only a penny. How much have you got?'

'Two pennies,' I said, stuffing some sticks into the sack, having shaken off all the snow and frost.

'Oh good!' said my sister. 'So you can buy one too. There's a little round thing with a funny mouse in it, and you have to get the glass balls into its eyes. It's a penny too. You'll love that.'

The next day was pretty good because there was a thaw in the night, so that made it all right for our father and mother to be on time. I mean the O.M. would be able to get up the lane. So we all went out, well wrapped up with scarves and Wellingtons and gloves and everything, and stamped about at the end of the muddy lane between 2 o'clock and 3 o'clock, as our father had promised to be there, and Mrs Daukes kept running down her path and said we'd all perish from the cold but she never asked us to come into her parlour and that was because Mr Daukes was probably still unconscious with his bad head and bandages everywhere. So Lally said. And then, just as it was beginning to get dusk, because we had got past the shortest day, we saw the headlights, the little ones, of the O.M. as it turned left at Piggy Corner and started to climb up the hill. It was exactly ten past three, and we all started cheering and waving, except silly Flora. She had just about got over her sulking on account of the bindie-wood business, but didn't know about cheering her father and mother because she only had a father and he wasn't worth cheering for anyway.

And then the huffle and bustle, the kissing and laughing, and our mother looking so pretty all wrapped up in the big moleskin travelling-rug, with her leather helmet and huge great goggles. Our father always drove with the hood folded away. It was a 'sports car', he said, so it was suitable. But our mother didn't very much like getting her hair all blown everywhere, so that's why she had to wear the helmet, like my father. Hers was brown and his black, and they had gauntlet gloves and all the luggage was in the big box strapped at the back. Minnehaha was in his basket with the wire front, under the tonneau cover at the back, and I was told to carry him up first and let him have a sniff round the sitting-room, locked in, while we all unloaded the car and got our mother safely up to the house. She was a bit wobbly from the drive, and from not being very strong after her fall down the stairs.

But Lally steadied her up the path and we all helped carry the parcels and cases. Just as it got really dark and my father started to cover the car for the night by putting up the hood and slotting in the isinglass windows (I had to help, and it was a jolly cold and fiddly job, I can tell you), I said, very politely, 'Where is the tree, Papa?'

He straightened up and put his hands to his mouth and said, 'Oh! My god!', which was pretty awful, but he looked so worried that I pretended I hadn't heard what he said and just went on talking and screwing the things that held the windows down.

'I know the goose is there – Lally said it was a "giant of a bird" – and there was the box of crackers, because I saw the name in wriggly writing, but there isn't a tree.'

And there wasn't, and our mother was quite amused when we told her and said it really didn't matter, we'd do without a tree this year because there had been so many problems for our father to worry about. He just forgot it, and it wouldn't have fitted into the car anyway. We had Minnehaha, crackers, the goose, even the pudding from October, and we had *them*, safe and sound. So that seemed reasonable, and Lally brought in the tea and a big dish of buttery crumpets with a lid on, and so I just forgot the tree. Well, sort of.

Minnehaha had almost settled down by this time, of course. He was pretty old, and he knew the cottage, and so he just went poking about here and there, sniffing, and in the end he jumped up on my father's lap and sat looking about him, his ears rather flat to his head. Flora said, 'I think he's scenting your wee mice in the cage. Cats have a wonderful sense of smell, that's how they find their prey.'

I really did want to give her a bonk on the nose, but Lally gave me one of her looks, and I just shrugged, and Lally said the mice were miles away in the lean-to, on a high shelf, and that Minnehaha was too old to 'caper about mousing'. It was kind of her, but I wasn't altogether certain. I didn't like the flat ears bit. But, of course, he *could* just have been listening for strange sounds after our house in Hampstead. His tail was twitching slowly, and I felt a bit worried. But I *did* want to bonk Flora for putting the idea into his head.

The lean-to was a bit cold. It had a tin roof and wooden walls, and no curtains or anything at the windows to keep out the draughts. But the Weekend seemed all right up on its shelf, and I'd given them a good chunk of fresh apple, some corn and a big fistful of hay for their bedding. There was a good smell everywhere of not only onions and paraffin, but creosote and turpentine. There were sacks of potatoes, a big row of marrows, jars of gooseberries and greengages, rows of our father's painting things and canvases stacked in a corner, and a line of stone jars full of ginger beer and parsnip wine which our mother 'put up' at the end of every summer. I liked the lean-to very much. It was sort of outside the house but inside the house at the same time, because if you opened one door you were in the garden, and the other one opened right into the kitchen with the glowing range and the copper and all the dishes and pots and pans. It was really very decent.

We didn't have Christmas stockings now that we were more grown up. So even though I woke up early, even before Lally, because you could see there was no light round her door, there wasn't much point in being awake because of no Christmas stocking, which was a bit sad. I remembered feeling it in the dark, the nuts in the toe, the tangerine a bit squashy if you weren't careful, the interesting rustling of paper and the liquorice-strap (that was easy to tell by being flat *and* round), and the cracker wagging about at the top. It was pretty exciting, but now there was no stocking and no tree. I just hoped there were presents of some sort. I had asked for a theatre from Mr Pollock's shop in Hoxton, but I didn't suppose our father had had the time to go there, not if he forgot the tree.

So I went to sleep again, and only woke up when Lally gave me a push and said, 'Happy Christmas, and you, Miss Fernackerpan! Wake up! It's Christmas morning and your parents' tea to get. Bonnie Caledonia! Wake up! Happy Christmas!' And carrying her candlestick and her indoor shoes, she went off down the stairs. She was so bossy and busy that you just *had* to get up, and this morning there was no wooding to do, so we had to wash our faces and hands first off. We each had a bowl and a jug of freezing water, and a big slop pail, and shared the soap. So it was all a bit of a muddle, except the girls got dressed while I washed, and then I gave Flora the Lifebuoy, and then my sister took it. We poured the bowls into the slop bucket and I had to carry it down and empty it in the drain outside the lean-to.

In the kitchen, kettles were boiling, the goose was on the table looking very white and dead beside a carrier bag from MacFisheries. Lally said, don't touch, because it was full of innards and she needed them and we'd have to manage best we could about breakfast and clear ourselves places because she was up to her eyes. Anyway, we had boiled eggs, no porridge today, and toast and rhubarb and ginger jam.

Then we all had to go down to the Court to get the milk and some cream. Our mother came down to see how we all were, and get another cup of tea and make the stuffing for the MacFisheries goose. She looked pretty in her kimono with a huge gold dragon on the back, and when I asked where our father was she just shook her head and said she really didn't know. I was pretty sure she really did but wasn't saying. So we went down to the Court, not down Great Meadow, because it was all muddy and boggy and my sister said there were some cows down in the corner and Flora said she was scared witless of cows.

But I didn't take much notice of that because she was witless anyway, so how could she be scared out of something she hadn't got? We walked, sploshed really, down the lane, and the chalky water was gurgling and spilling down the ruts because of the thaw, and there was no sound except for our sloshing and the water burbling.

'You'd think the world had stopped just because it's Christmas Day. It feels so funny,' said Flora, who was pretty funny herself.

The dairy at the Court was very interesting because it was half underground and half not, so that it would never get warm even in the very hottest summer. And it never did. There were little ferns growing along under the big slate shelves where the bowls of buttermilk and whey, skimmed, and 'Today's' and 'Yesterday's' stood. Everything was usually covered in muslin because of the flies from the yard, only, not today, because it was so cold even the ferns had gone all limp. But Miss Barbara Aleford was fussing about the very moment we pushed open the door. Inside it smelled lovely and damp, earthy and then sweet from the milk, and she was pouring a big crock of new milk into the bowls with 'Today's' on them.

'Heigh ho! Heigh ho!' she cried loudly and set the big crock down with a crack on the slate shelf. 'Happy Christmas! Wonderful day! See you've got your cans with you and that doesn't leave me to guess you need some delicious new milk from my animals. Got it right?'

I said that was right and gave her the cans.

'Today's or Yesterday's? All the same to me. In this cold Yesterday's will do you just as well and you can come down tomorrow and get some Today's. Capital!'

The Dairy at the Court –

She was quite tall, with earphone things curled round the side of her head, and men's corduroy breeches and canvas gaiters, and Lally once said that she was a poor soul who was grieving for her fiancé who had gone missing in the war. But she was still waiting for him because, at any old time, she told Lally, he'd just turn up. He knew the way like the back of his hand, and his pipe and baccy pouch were still in the front parlour where he'd left them.

It was a bit difficult to think of Miss Barbara with a fiancé, and waiting so long in those awful breeches, and her big red hands and earphones and all, when perhaps the fiancé had just gone away somewhere. Like our grandfather who, our mother said, suddenly hop-skipped it off to South America without so much as a by-your-leave or even a kiss to his wife, and just never came back. Wrote some letters but never came back. Just went off. Perhaps our grandmother had got into a bit of a huff. People did do that and it could make you very disagreeable. My sister did it sometimes, and sometimes Lally.

Miss Barbara was ladling the Yesterday's into the milk cans and humming under her breath. 'Bring your white mice again? Remember last summer and the harvest mice? Terrible that was! You got so upset . . .'

I remembered the harvest mice all right. I'd brought them back to the farm from the gleaning and they'd jumped out of my pocket and Miss Barbara had trodden on one in her huge old boots and killed it dead. So of course, I got upset, anyone would. Silly woman. So that's why I bought Sat and Sun in a pet shop in Lewes, to make up for it. Being dead, I mean. I said yes, they were in the lean-to and very well, thank you, and she ladled the milk and said that Mrs Daukes, up the top, had told her that my mother was not so well, on account of she had a nasty fall down the stairs not long ago ... and how sorry she was if she'd lost it ... and then she went quite red in the face and told me not to mind. Which I didn't. Grown-ups are very peculiar sometimes. Really ...

When we put the lids on the milk cans and thanked her, she wrote down what we owed on a slate on the wall and said, 'Take your mama some nice brown eggs, a present from me, help to build her up.' As if she was a castle or something. Still, it was very kind, and she put them in a brown paper bag with *Eat more fruit* on it, and gave it to Flora to carry, on account of we had the cans. Then we all called, 'Happy Christmas', and shuffled about on the wet stone floor and went out into the slushy yard. All the way to the lane we could hear her singing – well, that's what she would have called it – 'If I Had a Talking Picture of Youhoooo'. She was really a bit batty.

Our father was in the lean-to when we got back. He was looking very nice, wearing his painting smock which Mr Dick, the shepherd, had given him, and he smelled of turpentine. He had a saw in one hand and a clump of mistletoe which he'd cut from the old apple tree in the orchard. He held it over Flora's head and said we had to have a bit of mistletoe in the house so that he could kiss all the girls, and Flora made a soppy face and gave him the eggs instead.

Inside, the kitchen smelled of roasting goose and gravy, and the range was red hot and the copper boiling with steam tumbling about, and our mother, in a cotton frock, was getting the chestnuts ready for the sprouts. Everyone was very happy, busy and cheerful. You'd never know we had forgotten the tree. Our father hung the mistletoe in the door between the kitchen and the hallway and Lally said it would be a terrible nuisance there and couldn't we have it in the dining-room, over the table, and he said well, how could he kiss them all if it was over the table unless they all got on it? Anyway, Lally won, as usual. So he nailed it to a big beam above the table in the Big Dining-Room, which we never really used except for parties or Christmas. The door to *their* sitting-room was shut, and locked, and we had to go and take off our Wellingtons and coats and things and then he called to our mother, 'Margaret! I think it's high time for the presents, don't you?' and Lally and our mother came into the hall, and our father took off his smock and opened the sitting-room door.

And there it was.

The most beautiful tree you've ever seen. All gold and silver. Shining in the firelight. And we all cried out in surprise, and our father said the only thing was not to touch it really, because it was all made of holly branches and he'd had to paint all the leaves gold and silver by hand and it had taken him half the night. Our mother said that was his punishment for forgetting the tree in the first place, and Lally said it was a good thing she wasn't about to do any washing because her clothes' prop was now covered in holly and thick as a hedgehog with nails, and our father said there was quite a gap in the fence down at the Daukeses' cottage. Then they had sherry. Even Lally had a sip, but not too much on account of she'd be tipsy taking the goose out of the oven. All round the gold and

silver tree were the presents, including Flora's haggis –
you could tell them easily because they were round and
wrapped in tartan paper, and there was a huge box for me
and I knew what it was by shaking it. It was the Pollock's
Theatre. So they hadn't forgotten after all. And they had
made the tree.

After we'd opened all the presents our parents went
down to the village to telephone *The Times*. You always
had to telephone *The Times* to check that everything was
all right and that nothing terrible had happened in some
place like the Sahara or Berlin. You never could be certain,
our father said, that some 'idiot' hadn't got himself assassin-
ated or pushed off a cliff, and that really meant just
'killed' in simple English. But he had to 'check in'. So they
did, on Christmas morning even, from the Star at the
Market Cross because it had a telephone. Lally said *nothing*
stopped for *The Times*, it was all go.

I hoped, with my fingers crossed, that nothing awful
had happened when they telephoned, because if it had, that
meant our father would rush back to London no matter
what. So no Christmas dinner. I just prayed there wouldn't
be another airship crash, like the R.101, or another Em-
peror crowned in Abyssinia. Things like that got in the
way. But it was all right, and they came back safe and
sound. When I asked them, my mother laughed, looking
so pretty with sparky eyes and said no, nothing to make
our father go to *The Times*, just a bit of trouble in the
Punjab but then there always was, so we'd have a decent
time and dinner was at three o'clock on the dot.

It was terrifically busy at Euston Station: everyone in the

world seemed to be going to Scotland. All you could see was hundreds of people, and all you could hear was clangs and rattles and doors slamming and steam hissing and the scuff-skoff and clickety-clack of feet on the platform. Everyone was in a terrible hurry. Except us, because Lally said you always had to allow time for journeys and those sorts of things.

Flora was rather pale and didn't say much, and even at the bookstall, which was pretty exciting, she only nodded when she was asked if she'd like this or that for the journey. So she ended up with a copy of *Everybody's* and *Pip, Squeak and Wilfred*. And, just as Lally was putting her change away in her purse, there was our mother, and her best friend, Aunt Freda (who wasn't kith or kin but almost), who had a pointy nose, lots of rings, and came from Ireland. She also gave you jolly decent presents at Christmas and birthdays – like money.

'Found you at last!' said my mother. 'What a crowd, and you are fearfully early. But perhaps that's just as well.' And then she told Flora a lot of things about love to people, and to write a card when she was safely back, and hoped she'd had a lovely time with us and that we had been kind to her. And everyone agreed. I mean, standing among all those people by the bookstall, what could you do?

Lally adjusted her hat, put her bag under her arm, and I picked up Flora's suitcase, which wasn't very heavy really, in spite of all the presents we'd given her. Our mother said that she and Aunt Freda were off to Gunter's for coffee, because they hated goodbyes, and then they'd go off to the Caledonian Market, which was their favourite thing to

do, and which they did once a month. With a lot of kisses
and hugs and rearranging of veils and fur collars they
went away, waving like anything, until we couldn't see
them. All that was left was a smell of scent and face-
powder, and that didn't last long.

At the compartment door Flora said she'd take her case,
but I got in and put it on the rack. There was a quite nice
lady on one side and a fat man with a pipe who looked
over his glasses and rustled his paper on the other. But
they looked kind. Flora had tears running down her face.
I mean she wasn't crying, not making any sound, and her
face not screwing up or anything, just the tears down
her cheeks. Lally got out her handkerchief but Flora shook
her head and wiped her face with her gloved hands.

'Don't cry, Flora dear. All good things have to come to
an end, you know? And you'll soon be back. In the
summer perhaps . . .'

And Flora just said, in a sort of choky voice, 'I haven't
got one, you see?'

'Haven't got what?' said Lally, looking worried in case
she'd lost her ticket. But it wasn't that, and she said after a
big sniff, and another wipe, that she hadn't got a mother.
That made us feel rather awful, but Lally said well, you
have got brother Alec and your father and she was sure
they would be simply longing to see her again, and they'd
be at Central Station, Glasgow, to meet her.

But Flora just shook her head miserably. 'You are lucky.
You are so *lucky*, you two. You have one of each and I've
only got the one and he's always away fishing or sailing or
shooting or something.'

No one knew what to say, but thank goodness there

was a sudden moving about and doors started slamming, and a guard came hurrying along calling out and looking at his pocket watch like the White Rabbit. Lally said it was time to get on the train, and we all did a bit of kissing, only Flora's face was still wet and a bit sticky, and she was holding *Everybody's* and the Annual. The Guard slammed the door, and took his flag in his other hand, still looking at his watch, and Flora called down and said she was sorry, that she'd had a great time, that she'd never forget us all, or the cottage and her 'wee' room, and that we were very, very lucky.

As the train started to move slowly away, she waved and waved and it got faster and faster, and then she'd gone to Scotland, and we walked slowly through the people, and there was one woman crying, and a porter pushing a trolley and Lally said we had to mark her words.

'You're both very lucky children. Both very lucky indeed.'

That's what she said. So.

PART TWO

Chapter 6

If I turned my head to the left everything was pretty blurry, on account of all the grasses, very close to my face. And then, a bit further on, it all got speckled with blue, that was the scabious, then strips of red, and that was sorrel, and there was a quite big ant waggling up, his feelers waving about. If I turned my head and looked straight upwards it was all blue. Huge blue nothing. Not even a cloud . . . it just seemed to sparkle if you stared at it long enough. Our father said that was infinity. It's jolly far.

Then if I looked to my right, I saw my sister's head, and she was lying on her front, her fringe falling over her face so that all I could really see of her was her poky nose. But I knew she was fiddling at something, because her hair was swinging about and now and again (and this bit almost made me laugh out loud), you could see her pointy tongue flicking out. So there was her nose, her hair falling about, and her tongue flicking in and out like a grass snake. Only I didn't say so because she's petrified of snakes and when we come up here to the top of Windover she stamps through the grass because she says the vibrations will frighten away anything vile. She means snakes of course. Adders and so on. Even nice old slow-worms.

'What are you doing?'
'I'm saving its life.'
'What's life?' So I rolled over on my front because it was quite interesting to know what she was saving.

Couldn't be a snake and it couldn't be a beetle: she's not very fond of beetles either. I don't know, sometimes, why she doesn't live in *Hampstead* all her life. It was a pretty fiddly job, whatever it was she was doing, I could tell. And very slow and careful. Like peeling off a transfer.

'It's a poor little moth-thing. All wrapped up in a spider-web, and I'm going to save its life.'

'If it's all wrapped in cobweb it'll be too late. It'll be dead anyway.'

'No. Oh no. Sometimes the spider just wraps things up, like parcels, and keeps them in its web for later. Spider's larder. Only this poor thing isn't going to be eaten.' She cupped a sort of mummy-looking thing in her hand. It was all grey with web, but here and there you could see a bit of black and a little piece of red, so it had been a burnet moth or something. I mean 'had been' because it was as dead as anything. You could see that easily. Only she couldn't.

'Dead,' I said. 'All its juices have been sucked out. That's what spiders do, you know that. They wrap up the victim and then *suck* out the juices.' I said it twice because I liked the sound it made saying it.

My sister suddenly sighed. 'Oh look! Now see what you've done! Just because you are old Mister Know-All you've made me nervous and look what's happened! It's all broken.' She was holding some ashes, like off a cigar butt, in her hand. 'It would have been all right if you hadn't worried me with all that sucking part.' She threw the dusty pieces into the grass.

I told her that it wasn't my fault at all. It was a dead old moth and had been sucked empty and that it had just been hanging in the web in the hot sun, so what else could she expect? Dead as a door knob. And she started to brush down her cotton shorts and asked why door knobs were always dead when they were never alive in the first place. I said I didn't actually know, and sat up, resting on my elbows.

Far below, right beyond Long Barrow, you could see all the elms, still and dark in the sunlight, marking the lane down to Milton Street, and in Milton Street the squinty red roofs of the village and one, a bit bigger and in the middle, had 'The Friar's Head' painted in big white letters across the tiles. That was where we had to go for the bread, because there was a bake-house behind the pub and Winnie Moss did a bake on Wednesdays. Today was Wednesday, and we had to get a honeycomb as well, and Bert Moss, who ran the Friar's Head, kept bees and was pretty famous for his honey, and I was just hoping that the coppers which Lally had given me to pay for the loaf (best brown I had to ask for), and the comb, hadn't fallen out of my pocket, lying about in the grass. But it was all right actually, I had wrapped them in a piece of last week's *Larks*, so they made a bulgy packet and I could feel them through the flannel of my shorts.

So that was all right. We half ran, half walked in a sort of staggery way down the front, the very front, of the Long Man. I went down his left leg and my sister went down his right one, but we never trod on his face part. There wasn't a face really, just the outline, but it felt rather rotten to do that. We did once see one of those awful hiker people sliding down his face, or the place where his face *would* have been, and my sister was so

The Long-Man.

angry she actually shouted, 'Hoy! *Don't* do that!' The man looked a bit startled and when we began reaching down for handfuls of rabbit droppings to throw at him he hurried off down with his rucksack bumping about, and a fearful woman in a pink shirt and a beret shook a stick at us but she went off with him, so that was pretty good. We had to pick up rabbit droppings because there wasn't anything else – no flints (which would have really hurt them) but perhaps they thought they *were* flints, or stones anyway, and didn't realize they were only dried-up droppings.

We went down the Giant's legs because if you tried to go down the staffs, one in each hand, it was too narrow and steep. On his legs the earth was chalky and weedy. Too weedy, our father said, and one day, what with all the sheep and these wretched hiker people clambering around, there probably wouldn't be a Long Man, or a Giant, left. He said he'd put it in *The Times* and make a fuss. But anyway, we went down the legs (which was really forbidden) and into the gully at the bottom and then across the cornfield, through the gate and into the lane, just as old Mr Lush came slowly past on his tricycle like a big old stag beetle. He lived up in Wilmington. He'd lived up in Wilmington all his life and had never been anywhere else, except once when he'd gone down to Hastings after the Boer War. He was too old to be in our father's war, so he just stayed where he was in Wilmington and did some thatching and pruned his orchard and went on his tricycle from time to time to the Friar's Head, where he had a special seat which was all shiny from his bottom. He was always in black: a black suit, black cap, black gaiters and black boots. He never wore a collar or anything like that, just a red handkerchief with white dots on it. You could see him for miles because he always rode in the middle of the road, and he was perched quite high up on the tricycle, so you really couldn't miss him. The carters got pretty fed up with him because he was slower even than their horses, and sometimes when a car came along they honked and honked but he took no notice because he was stone deaf. Lally said that one day someone would lose their patience and he'd end up in a ditch. Dead. But he said to Winnie Moss, who told me, that he liked to have a lot of space right and left of him when he was riding on account of he didn't want to scratch the paint off his tricycle on the hedges. I mean, you couldn't argue with a man who had only been to *Hastings* once in his whole life.

We waved to him and he nodded at us but he didn't take his hands off the handlebars in case he fell off. We were ahead of him, so if he was going to the Friar's Head, and it was about the right time in the morning, we'd get there first, thank goodness.

'He hasn't even got a cycle lamp!' said my sister. 'Did you notice? No cycle lamp, it's terribly dangerous.'

'I bet he never goes out at night, or in the dark. He wouldn't dare, being deaf and so slow ... and it's a good mile from Wilmington.'

'If the policeman saw him I bet he'd get a good wigging.'

'He's too famous. No one would dare touch him.'

'That Mr Hitler would. Lally's one. She never says, "I'll fetch a policeman if you don't behave." Remember? Years ago when we were little? Now it's always this Mr Hitler, who isn't a *bit* frightening. But her brother Harold, he's a policeman, and he's *very* frightening. He's huge *and* frightening.'

She walked along nodding her head and muttering away to herself. I walked on beside her thinking how hot it was and why my plimsolls were starting to rub my heel, and then it was all right because we were in front of the pub, and went through the gate into the yard where Winnie Moss was hanging out some tea towels. Winnie Moss was very nice, with round glasses and elastic stockings. She flapped dry one of the towels with *Glass* printed on it and said she knew what we were there for, and that she'd taken her bake out of the oven and it was cooling, and, talking of cooling, would we like a glass of Eiffel Tower lemonade? She wouldn't be a tick.

We sat down on some empty crates in the shade. There was a lovely smell of spilled beer, yeast and washing. Then Bert Moss pushed open the gate carrying a big trug basket full of new potatoes. He had a fork in one hand, so we knew he'd been in the vegetable garden, and he waved it at us and said that Ben Lush had just arrived so he couldn't stop for a chat but he'd be back as soon as he'd got Ben settled. He stamped his feet on the mat outside the kitchen door to get the earth off his boots, just as Winnie Moss came out with a jug of water and two glasses and the bottle of Eiffel Tower lemonade powder and a spoon in the pocket of her pinafore.

'I reckon Miss Jane wants her honey like usual? I'll tell Albert. He's got me some 'taters and here's the lemonade.'

Bert Moss pushed his cap to the back of his head and scratched his ear. You could see he was a bit fussed because he just dumped the muddy fork against the door jamb and clods of chalky earth fell off, and he said, 'I know as *I'm* out here and *you* are out here, but who is minding, I'd very much like to know?'

Winnie Moss was spooning out the lemonade powder into the glasses set on an empty crate. 'Enid is minding the bar. Now, you two, don't want it too strong, do you? Too acidy.' And she filled the glasses with water from the jug while Bert Moss grumbled off into the house. 'You want another glass, and you're welcome. Here is the bottle and one teaspoon.' Then she hurried after Mr Moss calling out to him not to drop muck all over her brickwork because she had just Ronuk'd it and we had need of a honeycomb. Then it was all quiet, and I unlaced my plimsolls to rub the blistery part on my heel. My sister was sitting sipping her yellow lemonade very slowly. She said that if you drank too quickly in the heat you could have a heart attack and die. And why was it so yellow and the lemonade our mother and Lally made was sort of grey? I didn't know, except that Eiffel Tower brand, in its little square bottle, was probably French and very expensive. She said that if it was you wouldn't get it at the Friar's Head because our father said it was a cheap sort of pub. And not really as good as the Star in the market square. So it stood to reason. I didn't argue because I didn't really know what standing to reason meant. Neither did she, but she'd heard grown-ups use it and thought it would be a jolly good shut-up. Which it was. Winnie Moss came back wiping the flour off her hands with the 'best brown' in a paper bag and said to tell Miss Jane that all she was baking now was best brown and no white, never no more, and to leave this one to settle a bit before cutting. It was just out of the oven, and the door of the oven was wide open, to cool it, and you could see the curve of the pink bricks and smell the crustiness and wood ash.

'Upon my soul,' she said. 'I really did do a baker's dozen today, one over the odds, but there's a big order from over at Arlington. I do believe there's a wedding,. maybe a funeral. Anyway, no one we know, so no need to fret. And paid in advance, which will go a long way to getting Mr Moss his fourth hive. Quite taken up with honey, he is.'

Then Bert Moss came back, and took the fork. He was wearing a pair of slippers and had the honeycomb wrapped up in a bag. 'Mind how you go with this, it'll run everywhere if you crack it. Tell your farthar it's the usual old blend as he says. Thyme, gorse, clover and goodness knows what else. We haven't seen him, not all this summer?' I said no, because he was visiting in Germany with my mother, and Bert Moss stopped scraping the mud off the prongs and said that was very interesting. I told him that they'd gone to look at some new machines for printing newspapers and he wanted to buy them for *The Times*. So he wouldn't be at the cottage except perhaps for a week, later on. Bert Moss asked where he was in Germany because he had been a prisoner of war himself and was he anywhere near where he had been. I didn't know. I mean, you *do* get asked difficult questions by people. But my sister, always trying to be a bit showy-offish, said she couldn't remember the name *exactly* but it was the same as the scent that people put on their handkerchiefs when they had a cold or a bad headache. Bert Moss just looked

The Star Inn.

worried and said he'd never heard of a German town called Vick, but after all he'd only been a prisoner.

Then Winnie Moss came out and said that the money I'd given her was exact to the ha'penny, and did my sister mean Cologne. And we both remembered that that was right. It was hopeless walking home with my sister, she was so sarcastic and pleased with herself because she had remembered the rotten place and I had forgotten. But honestly, who would remember a name like Cologne? Unless they had headaches or something. So I just carried the honeycomb carefully and didn't speak. Not one single word. And serve her right. Only she just went on singing 'All the King's Horses', but she didn't know all the words, so she just la-la'd all the way back until we got to Great Meadow and turned into the field. And I really would have quite liked to have given her a terrific bonk on the head.

But I didn't.

It really was so hot that we ducked under the trailing brambles and old man's beard at the start of the gully and walked up to the cottage in the cool, speckly shade. My heel hurt a bit, so I took off my plimsolls because I knew where all the stony bits of the path were, so that was all right. My sister had stopped singing about all the King's horses and all the King's men, thank goodness. But I could tell she was having a good think. I knew that because she was biting away at her bottom lip, and that was never a good sign. She was working something out, and when she asked could she carry the honeycomb, I knew that her think would be a bit worrying.

'I've been carrying this ever since we left the Friar's

Head. Hours ago. *Now* you say you'll carry it! Just when we can see the roof of the cottage! We are almost home.'

'Well, I asked you . . .'

'You are *hinting*.'

'You are vile! I won't say another word. Not another.' And she tripped over a bit of dead tree. 'Not a word. And it was something lovely. For you.'

'What was?'

'My think.'

'Well, say then. Go on. Say. What? Tell.' I was getting a bit puffed and the sweat was running down my back. I knew I *should* be thinking 'perspiration' but I was too tired. So I just thought 'sweat'.

'Well, you remember that dear little shell-thing I got in the crackers at Christmas?'

'No.'

'You do!'

'Do not. Don't remember. What little shell-thing?'

'A dear little Japanese shell and when you drop it into a tumbler of water it just bursts open, and the most lovely, amazing flowers start growing. Just in a tumbler of water. Really magic flowers. You do remember? We had them last year too, only this year I got it.'

I did remember, of course, as soon as she said it, but I was hot and a bit fed up because then all I had got was a wooden whistle and a paper hat. But I was sure she had opened her shell and put it in water already, so there was no need to show her that I was interested. So I didn't bother. I just shrugged and said I bet she had already used it up.

'I haven't, I *haven't*! It's still in the shell, all shut. With a bit of sticky paper covered in squiggly writing. Our father says it's Japanese.'

'Well, so what about it? That was at Christmas, now it's July. Perhaps it's gone off, or something, and it's too hot to argue and my heel hurts.'

'You and your old heel. But what I was thinking was that *if* I gave you my sweet little Japanese shell, *for keeps*, we could go down to Baker's and buy one big bottle of Tizer. Just for us! Wouldn't you love that? I mean *wouldn't* you really? A big cold Tizer?'

You see? So awful. Really cheaty. She was so secret. So I said I thought it was a rotten idea, and that if she wanted a whole bottle of Tizer why didn't she go down to the village and buy herself one. Mind you, I knew that she never would. Not on her own, on account of the heifers down in the corner, only, she thought they were bulls, all swishing their tails and putting the fear of death into her. She was quiet for a bit, chewing her lips, as we started up the slope at the end of the gully, and Great Meadow was all yellow with buttercups. I put on my plimsolls again and she said, shaking her head in a waggly way, that she hadn't any Saturday money left, she'd spent *hers*, and all she had left was her 'sweet little shell, *unopened*'.

I *ask* you! You do see what I mean? A real cheat. So I said, holding the honey very carefully and starting for the garden fence, 'I've only got threepence left of my Saturday money, and I'm saving that up for the August Fair, so that is that.'

'Threepence! That's all we *need*! Threepence, and I'll give you my dear little shell in exchange!'

'I don't want your rotten old shell from Christmas!'

She began to whine again, like they do, and said it was too hot, and she began to scuff through the buttercups and things, which meant that she'd get her socks all runkled and grass-stained, and a good ticking-off from Lally. If we ever got home.

As we started clambering over the rickety iron fence by the privy, she said in a sad soppy voice, 'Fancy not wanting that *dear* little shell. You could afford it, easily. And then we could have all the Tizer together and not share with anyone, and we could both watch the lovely flowers opening. Together. I mean, it *is* sharing, isn't it?'

And I said to shut up and there was a lot of ginger beer in the kitchen. She huffed and puffed and pulled the heads off some cow parsley and threw them up in the air.

'Tizer is best. It's fizzy. And cool, and lovely. I think you are vile. And mean too. Mean and vile.'

And then she ran off down to the lean-to singing her 'All the King's Horses' song. I ask you. Trying to make me buy her rotten old shell for threepence when she had got it for nothing in a cracker. Girls are really quite rotten sometimes.

Because it was so hot we had only cold for lunch. Lally wore short sleeves, so you could tell how hot it was because she never would have worn short sleeves in the house, not ever.

It was going to be ham and potato salad and lettuce and half a tomato each. And there was a bottle of Heinz mayonnaise, only a titchy one, because my father didn't like anything in bottles, except if it was to drink, so they had to be hidden when he was at the cottage. Like the bottle of Daddies Sauce. But Lally said that when the cat's away the mice will play. That reminded me that I'd better give a bit of lettuce (the outside leaves) to the Weekend, which I had taken to the brick shelf halfway up the stairs on account of it was too hot in the lean-to. It was quite dark in the hallway, after the sunlight, and Lally called out to come and wash my hands, and I was just starting up the stairs when there was the most terrible clatter and something jumped right over my head and the whole Weekend went smashing to the ground and the glass just shattered and there was sawdust everywhere. I saw Sat and Sun running about quite terrified and heard Lally crying out, 'Oh! Oh! It's that dratted cat! Shoo, shoo!' But I was trying to catch the mice, only I couldn't. They were too fast and went scampering down the stairs, and Lally banged a saucepan to frighten Minnehaha out of his wits, and she frightened Sat and Sun too, but of course she didn't mean to do that. It was just all terrible. I stood in the hallway and she said had they escaped and I just chucked the bits of old lettuce into their broken cage and started to pick up the glass bits.

'It's a good job it's a cold lunch today. Get this cleared up. Sawdust and bits of carrot . . . I'll get you a bucket, and mind your hands – we don't want blood everywhere.'

So I just picked everything up, very slowly: the food bowl, the water bowl, the little wheel they used to exercise in, the straw from their nest. And it was all blurry, and I had to keep wiping my face, and my nose was running a bit. But I didn't make a noise or anything. It was no good looking for Sat and Sun because they had gone for good, and I'd never find them in all of Great Meadow. So that was that. Then I put everything into the bashed cage, and carried it and the bucket of glass to the kitchen. My sister said what a dreadful smell and she was having her lunch and Lally said, 'Outside with that, young man.' So I just wandered into the front garden and everything went a bit swimmy. I mean, I couldn't really see very well, but I didn't want them to notice in the kitchen, so I went right down to the Daukeses' hedge and emptied the glass right in the middle of it.

No one really cared. That was the worst part. They just sat there eating their cold ham and talking about going down to the post office after lunch to see if there were any letters and save the van a journey up the hill. And I just sat on a big flowerpot and looked at the broken cage and thought of all the happy times I'd had with Sat and Sun, just watching them really. When I thought of all the snow and ice in the winter and how terrible it would be for them I felt awful. And what was worst of all, I looked up, and sitting on the top of one of the posts in the fence was Minnehaha, looking all of a mess. Watching me. So I just chucked their food bowl at him. Hard. It didn't hit him, only the post, and it skipped off into Great Meadow and so did he. And I just sat. It was a really rotten morning.

Then I heard Lally coming down the path. I knew it was her because she was singing 'Moonlight and Roses' quite loudly. I knew she was singing loudly so I'd hear and have time to wipe any snot away, but there wasn't any. I don't blub so anyone can see. So that was all right.

'Well, so that's where you've got to!' she said, as if she didn't know all the time, because she could have seen me plain as plain from the window over the sink. But I didn't

1 The 'cottage', 1930. Rented for 7/6 a week.

2 My father, just after joining *The Times*, 1912.

3 With my parents at Sainte-Cécile, France, 1922.

4 At Wimereux, with my boat made by my father, 1926.

5 My sister posing for a 'Drink More Milk' campaign, about 1927.

6 With Mama on the beach at Deauville, 1926ish.

7 With the new Salmson, a French car which my father loved and drove at Brooklands. Summer, 1926.

8 The only existing 'snap' of Lally, with my sister. Cuckmere, 1930.

9 Mama at the annual Astor Garden Party for *The Times*. Hever Castle, 1927.

10 At Melrose Abbey, 1928.

11 My parents in the blue OM. This pre-dated the all-silver one.
1929–30.

12 An aerial view of the cottage and Great Meadow. Taken by my father in 1930.

say anything, and when she said, 'No lunch then?' I just shook my head, and she said that perhaps I'd better go and have a look for Minnehaha because he was in rather a state after jumping through the kitchen window and taking the fly-paper with him. We always had fly-papers hanging about the place, like long twisty strips of old apple peeling, and that was why he looked a bit of a mess sitting on the post. But I just shrugged. Lally said she couldn't stand about all day and that it would take hours to cut all his fur off and she wasn't about to do it so I'd better start looking for him, and by the by, she'd opened the last jar of our mother's own piccalilli and if I wanted some I'd better make haste before Miss Fernackerpan took the lot. So I got up. It was easier to do what she wanted than to sit there really. And it was a bit worrying about Minnehaha and the fly-paper. I'd have to cut all his fur off and that would be very difficult.

Walking up slowly through the rows of runner beans and the sprouting broccoli, Lally suddenly said, very nicely, 'I tell you what. When the parents come back from Germany I shall have a week off to see Mr and Mrs Jane, Friday to the following Monday, and I wonder if you would both like to come with me? You'd have to share the big bed, like always, but I reckon, if you'd like to come, the parents would be delighted to get rid of you and be on their own. Would that cheer you up then?'

Well, she knew it would. After the cottage, Walnut Cottage, Twickenham, was the very best place in the world, so I quickly said yes before she changed her mind.

'Well, that's that. I'll drop Mrs Jane a postcard just to warn her . . .'

'About the Weekend, it's all my fault you know,' I said. 'Really, I mean. If *only* I had left them in the lean-to, and made a sort of umbrella-thing for shade, or *if* I'd made some more air holes, and *if* I hadn't put them on the shelf on the stairs, Minnehaha wouldn't have jumped up on them . . .'

'If "ifs" and "ands" were pots and pans, there'd be no need for tinkers!' said Lally. 'No use fretting. You come and have a bit of Mr Wilde's home-cured and then, quick sharp, go and find that dratted cat.'

But no sign. I called and called and called. Nothing. I went to all the places I knew he might have been, lying rolled up in fly-paper, at the back of the privy, in the nettlebed by the rubbish heap, even up in the churchyard behind the Well Beloved and Departed This Life stones, but no. Not a sign anywhere. Not a meow, not a whimper. It was very worrying. But Lally told me to get-a-move-on-do, and while she was adjusting her white halo-hat (only used for Best or Hampstead – there was a black one for funerals or the theatre) she said he'd very likely come back in the cool of the evening, when he got a bit hungry. And not to forget to wear our 'hates', awful cotton things we had to wear because of sunstroke (I ask you), and that she was only wearing her white because her beret was red, and she didn't want all those heifers, or cows, to come calumping up to her and giving her a terrible turn in all this heat, which would do for her.

'I've never forgotten those terrible great eyes, rolling about in those huge heads, and all that spittle dribbling down from their frothy mouths! A terrible turn that was.

Don't tell me they aren't mad. Stark staring mad, and I *attract* them. Anything red and I'm done for, anything. Come along now, do . . . we'll keep to the lane side of the hedge down to the Court. Got the basket?'

It was lovely and cool and shadowy in Wilde's the grocer's, and quite peaceful except for all the wasps zooming about the Demerara sugar drawer and the South African sultanas like angry swallows. A lot of them got stuck on the spirals of fly-paper all over the shop, and that was a bit rotten because it reminded me of Minnehaha, but Mr Wilde said he'd be stung to death if he didn't deal with the 'wapsies' (that was his name for them). Miss Maltravers, who was sitting in her little cage-thing up at the end of the shop (and serve her right, she was such a Nosey Parker), kept fanning herself with a pad of postal orders, and the draft jiggled all the fly-papers round her scales, and fluttered the papers on her counter so she had to put tins of pineapple chunks on them to keep them from blowing about the shop.

'Well, I do declare! Miss Jane! And you don't often grace our premises, more is the pity for us here.'

'Too much to do up the top. These children would run wild given half a blink. The cat's got caught in the fly-paper. *He's* lost his white mice. And I don't know what next. I'll have a three-ha'penny stamp please, Miss Maltravers.'

'It's for Great Britain I take it?' She was tearing a little stamp very delicately out of her big stamp-book. 'No one abroad? Because, as you know, Miss Jane, that comes extra.'

'I don't know anyone abroad except a cousin in Hayling

Island, and I believe that is still in Great Britain even though it's an island. Am I correct?'

'You certainly are! It all belongs to King George, and that's a comfort even if they do say he's really a German. But, you see, a *diluted* German. That takes the fizz out of them, if you follow.'

Then, after thanking us, she began fanning herself again and Lally read out her list of things for tomorrow and we posted the letter in the box in the wall just outside the shop. So that was that. Tomorrow Mrs Jane would get the good news that she'd have to get the big bed ready and aired in the little room looking over the back garden and the old pear, and very likely, if we were really lucky, we'd have Gravesend shrimps and whelks and winkles for tea. And that would be the very best thing of all, with bread and butter and a homemade raspberry sponge after.

Going down Sloop Lane to the river and the bridge, Lally told me to carry the basket while she counted the change in her purse. 'There it lies!' she said. 'I was wondering about that spare ha'penny. Never can be sure, they sweep them up before your very eyes. A penny ha'penny for a postcard . . . I ask you!'

'You put it in an envelope, so it went like a letter,' I said.

'I know I did. Postcards are for everyone to read, and Miss Maltravers has gimlet eyes, as we all know, and I am not about to have her spreading it all over the village that I have my week off soon, and please to make me an appointment at the barber's, and that you'll both be coming with me. That's our affair. Anyway, I had to let Mother know: can't give her a Scarborough warning, can

I, not with three of us and the big bed to air. She's not a girl any longer. Oh no . . .'

'What's a Scarborough warning?'

'I don't know, so don't ask, but I don't want to give her one. All I know is they can give you a regular fright. Ask no questions, you'll hear no lies . . .'

So I shut up, and we all crossed the white bridge over the Cuckmere.

Chapter 7

The long shed at Walnut Cottage went all down the brick garden wall. The roof was just ripply tin, and one side, looking on to Mrs Jane's drying-lawn and the big pear tree, was all windows. Different sorts of windows, joined together, which Mr Jane had collected from places where he had worked. Inside, it was dusty and dim, because the windows were cobwebby. There was a long work-bench nicked and scarred with saw marks, and rusty tins of paint and creosote. It smelled of winter onions and corn for the hens, wrinkled apples and boxes of shallots. Up on the brick wall there was a snarling fox mask, which terrified my sister, who said that it watched her wherever she went, and sneered at her. It couldn't possibly because it was just a mask, just an old head, stuck on a wooden shield. There was a stuffed pike and some perch, with orange fins, which I rather liked, and a big set of wooden drawers, but quite small ones, with printed labels on them saying 'Hinges' or '1/2 in. Screws' or 'Tacks' and that sort of thing. Mr Jane was very tidy when he wasn't being forgetful, which Mrs Jane said was getting more and more 'frequent'. I think she meant more often.

He was setting a lot of things down on the work-bench and I had to say what they were. It was a bit boring, but he was very nice really and he said I had to know how to 'handle things'. I didn't much want to, but I was a guest after all. So.

'What's this then? This thing?'

'A spoke-shave.'

'Yers. And this?'

'A hammer.'

'Ar . . . but what kind of hammer? Got to be clear.'

'A claw-head hammer?'

'Is right. This yere . . .?'

'I don't know. Yes I do. A kind of saw . . .'

'If you know, *what* saw is it?'

'Jig.'

'Got 'im. And this yere? Different saw, you know it?'

'Yes. For keyholes.'

'And this then, what about this?'

And it was a small box-thing, with spotty brown paper on its back, and a lot of dust, and when I turned it round it was the most marvellous thing I'd ever seen. Well, for a very long time. Since we'd arrived anyway. It had two stuffed voles in it. Real, but dead. Little water voles, and they were sitting on a piece of paper riverbank stuff, with tufts of dried grasses and a bit of fern, and one vole was poking its head out of a hole, and the other was eating a nut or something. It was really terrifically exciting. I mean, they looked so real and everything.

'What's them then?'

'They are voles. Water voles. Stuffed.'

'Yers. See the date, down the bottom? Fallen off, has it?'

He sounded anxious, but it was all right because it hadn't fallen off, it was just a bit squinty, and it said, in gold letters, 'Pair of common voles. May '88'. Mr Jane said a friend of his did a bit of stuffing in the old days and this pair had been taken down at Strawberry Hill before all the building had started. But then it was just fields and only the park when he was a lad. He said he was sorry to hear that my pets had 'gorn', and would I like to have the voles because he didn't want them and Mrs Jane wouldn't have them in the house because of fleas or bugs. I thought it was very decent of him to think of Sat and Sun and to give me the voles, and I shook his hand and thanked him. He smelled of cough-drops, even though it was summer, and then blew the dust off the glass case and said it was mine. So I took it and went off to the house to show everyone and just when I got into the yard the yard door opened and someone came in pushing a bike and holding the door into the front garden wide open. Then it slammed shut and Mr Jane said who was that young chap banging around? And it wasn't a young chap at all. It was Lally. With no hair. Well, anyway, not much. We just stood staring down the yard, and she waved, and leant her bike against the walnut tree. She smoothed down her skirt and then, of course, you could see it was not a 'young chap' at all.

I asked what had she done, and she said, 'To what, pray?'

Mr Jane said, 'Your 'ead is what. Wait till Mother sees what you gone and done.'

And Lally said she was over twenty-one and she liked it and where was the mirror in this house?

So it was a bit boring really. I mean, *now* no one was interested at all in my voles and my sister made a sort of gasping sound and said, 'Oh! What's happened? What did you do?' to Lally, who was poking bits of hair round her ears and she said she'd 'merely had my hair cut'.

Then Mrs Jane came into the scullery where we all were and gave a terrible screech, and it was just one word, 'Nelly!', very loud indeed. That was pretty terrible because 'Nelly' was really Lally's family name, only, no one ever called her that unless it was truthfully serious. So this was.

'What *have* you done, girl?' said Mrs Jane standing at the kitchen door with a colander of runner beans.

'I've had my hair cut, Mother. You knew I was going to the Salon Elite, I asked you to make the appointment. Over at the Green.'

'I can't believe it! Bless my sister's cats! You look just like a boy!'

And Lally just looked at herself in the mirror over the sink and smiled and smiled and said she knew that, it was all The Thing. You could see Mrs Jane was vexed, or worried, or something, because she just pushed Lally aside and set the colander in the sink and turned on the tap very fast, and you could see she was angry. And Lally said that *everyone* is doing their hair this way now, it was cooler and easier to manage. And Mrs Jane said, 'Manage! I'll give you manage, my girl – with the back of my hand if you weren't over age!'

Lally said that she *was* over age so leave it be. Mrs Jane grumbled and rinsed the beans, and my sister and Mr Jane went out into the yard together. I was just hoping and hoping that there would be a quiet time when I could show the voles to someone. But no one was interested, so I didn't. Mrs Jane turned off the tap and asked whoever looked like that in Twickenham, she'd like to know. And Lally said, 'Oh! Mother, do give over. Gooze next door looks like this.'

Mrs Jane said that Gooze-Next-Door was soft in the head, and had been all her life, and if that's how Lally wanted to look, that's just how she did.

So I just took my voles and went back to the long shed, where I could hear them all talking away like anything. It was pretty mouldy really: no one cared about my present or how kind it was of Mr Jane to think of Sat and Sun and that sort of thing. So I found a piece of rag and cleaned the glass front, and polished it up a bit, and I heard my sister shouting away at Mr Jane as they came down the path from the greenhouse.

'I bet you will never guess what!' she said, and her face was all smiley and secret-looking, so I said I was busy cleaning the vole box so I could take it into the house and then she said (quite nicely actually), 'Mr Jane has given me a whole bunch of grapes. He put a piece of red string round a bunch and said that it was mine. When they are ripe. *My* bunch is the red one. Wasn't that very *sweet* of him?'

So I said yes, and found a hole in the spotty brown paper on the back of the stuffed voles. Which was quite interesting, because if I could find a mothball I could drop one in, and then there would be no fleas or bugs and I'd be allowed to take it up to our room. So that cheered me up, and I was quite curious watching Mr Jane, who was opening some of his little wooden drawers full of screws and tacks and three-inch nails. Looking for something. I wondered if he had any mothballs. I mean, you never know.

My sister suddenly said, 'I told Mr Jane that you would like a bunch of grapes too. From Hampton Court. So he's looking for the string to tie on *your* bunch. I told him you'd be very happy if you had one.' So, you see, she *was* pretty decent really. I mean, if you ever found out. It was quite difficult sometimes, but she did make me feel I really and truly liked her. So I said, 'Thank you,' and then asked Mr Jane if he had any mothballs. But he was a bit deaf and didn't hear so I shouted. My sister said, 'Don't shout he's not deaf, you *are* rude.'

But he was staring at me, with a ball of raffia in his hand. 'What say?' he called across the shed, so I said it again, and he shook his head and said to ask Mother. Then he said best go and have another look at the Hampton Court vine down at the greenhouse, and with a pair of scissors and the ball of raffia he wandered into the yard. We followed, only, I left the voles behind so they'd be safe. In the greenhouse he told me to choose my own bunch. I saw my sister's hanging up among the leaves with a long red wriggle of tape, so I chose one almost as big as hers, and Mr Jane tied a bit of the raffia round it. He was whistling under his breath and grunting a bit, but then it was done, and we looked at our bunches.

'End of October, I reckon. You'll have to come back at the end of October. From Hampton Court, they are. Took the cutting years and years ago. Afore I spoke for Mrs Jane even. Been here umpteen years.'

When we were walking back down the path to the long shed, my sister said that did I know that he had actually stolen the bit of vine from King Henry's Palace. And it was hundreds of years old. I told her she was pretty decent to have remembered to get me a bunch, but she just shrugged and said that if I hadn't a bunch of my own

I'd have to share hers, Lally would see to that. So it was much better if I had my own. So she could have all hers for herself.

You see? Pretty rotten really. Girls are.

We all had supper in the kitchen. It was still light outside, so there was no lovely lamplight or a fire in the range. Not until the Last Day of Summer. We had boiled eggs for supper, with fingers, and Mr Jane had some savoury mince at his little bamboo table by the empty range, which had two gas rings on the top so that we had two kettles sighing away for the tea or washing-up. Lally and Mrs Jane seemed to have said sorry, or something, because they were quite nice to each other, and Lally said that we were having the eggs for supper on account of we'd had some pilchards for lunch, and if we so much as whispered *that* to our father we'd never be allowed to come to Walnut again.

'He's so against anything in tins,' she said to Mrs Jane. 'Ptomaine poisoning, he says. You don't know how long the things inside have been dead.' Mrs Jane said, 'Oh well, bang goes my potted salmon. I thought of that for tomorrow, but what with pilchards today, and he's so against tinned things, it might be tempting fate.' So she'd think of a bit of salt beef and salad instead. Lally said that on Sunday she wouldn't be there, to keep an eye on things, so we could all have whatever we liked to eat and she wouldn't be witness. When she said that, Mrs Jane looked quite pale and said, where, pray, would she be on Sunday then? We were to stay until Monday? So what was she supposed to do, being left responsible for two energetic children, and Lally said she had it in mind to go to the Regal in Richmond to see Bebe Daniels.

Mrs Jane set her cup down with such a bang that it splashed the cloth with tea. Even Mr Jane looked up from his plate and said that, yes, he'd quite finished, Mother, and it was very nice thank you. Lally said that was what she was doing on Sunday afternoon tea-time, going to see *Rio Rita* with Bebe Daniels and, her favourite, John Boles.

This gave Mrs Jane the most terrible shock, and she got to her feet so quickly that she knocked the milk jug over and I stuck my spoon right through the shell of my egg.

'Father!' she shouted. 'Our Nelly has lost her mind!' When she reached to get his plate he said no, he didn't want no more, but a nice cup of tea when it was to hand.

'I don't know! I *really* don't know!' said Mrs Jane scraping the dirty plate with a fork and shaking her head. She looked so sad in her wraparound pinafore and her good shoes with the button straps, and her bun starting to squiggle down with all the head-shaking, and her pince-nez waggling. 'It's the Lord's Day. You can't defy the Good Lord, my girl. And get that milk mopped up quick sharp.'

You see, she could be just as bossy with her own daughter as her own daughter was with us.

But Lally was busy mopping up the milk anyway. 'There's no need to throw a fit, Mother! It's the law now. It's allowed, Sunday cinemas . . .'

Mrs Jane started to clear up her plate and cup and saucer and stack them on a tray. My sister and I just stayed quiet. It was a bit funny hearing the grown-ups being so angry with each other. Then Lally said that if we had finished our supper perhaps we would be very kind and go and

lock up the hens, and she'd give Mrs Jane a hand in the
scullery. Well, we had finished, and went down the path
to the hen run. The sun was just flickering over the roof
of the jam factory at the end of the garden and it was still
very warm and little spirals of gnats were dancing about
under the trees and the hens weren't really pleased about
being shut up, so we had to shoo them into their house
with a lot of flapping and my sister trod in their water
bowl, so that was another accident.

'Mrs Jane was really jolly cross. Did you see her bun?
All shaking loose, and the way her glasses were all glittery.
Like a terrible witch's. Awful!'

'Witches don't wear glasses,' I said.

'Well, you know what I mean anyway. And Mrs Jane is
so sweet and pretty, she couldn't be a witch really, but she
just seemed like one, she was so flustered.'

'Well, I do think it's a bit awful. Going to the pictures
on a Sunday, even if it *is* allowed.'

My sister bolted the hen house door and pushed the
half-empty water bowl under the stand-tap with her foot.
'Think of the germs too! Germy people everywhere.' She
turned on the tap. 'The "wrong sort" of people go to the
pictures on a Sunday. I know that. It's so wicked that only
really horrible people bother to go. No wonder Mrs Jane
was so angry.'

'Upset.'

'Well, upset then. No wonder. Germy people breathing
everywhere.'

'*We* weren't asked. So you needn't worry. She's going
all by herself, with no hair.'

'I'm not worried. I wouldn't go anyway, even if she did

ask us. Silly old Bebe Daniels and that soppy man. I wouldn't go. I'd be petrified. It's vile, that's what.'

But I don't think she really meant it. I didn't say anything, and we walked back to the house and they were still talking quite loudly. We could hear them easily by the outside lav and the old enamel bath used for rainwater, next to Mr Jane's show auriculas.

'I *really* don't know . . . everything is changing. I don't care if it is all The Thing to cut your hair off, and take a trolley bus, or whatever they call them, to Isleworth or Richmond, but I *do* care about the Lord's Day and His Rules, and I'm shocked. Very shocked in a daughter of mine. You wait till I tell Brother Harold. And Ruby. You wait, my girl.'

Well, we knew now she really was very angry because of the 'my girl' part, and it was pretty worrying about Brother Harold and his frizzy-haired wife Ruby, because he was jolly big and a policeman, and Lally wasn't very keen on him, we knew. Perhaps it might put her off?

But when we got into the kitchen she was setting all the washed-up cups and plates back on the dresser and Mr Jane was dozing and Mrs Jane was folding the tablecloth, and we didn't say anything. Then Mrs Jane said, had we shut the hen run, and we said yes, and she thanked us and put the cloth in the table drawer and tucked her hair back into her bun.

'Anyway, Mother,' said Lally, untying her apron at the back, 'anyway, I could have gone and never mentioned it. Said I was going over to Teddington to see Mavis and Dolly, never mentioned going to the Regal, and you'd have been no wiser. I could just have told a lie. You'd never have known.' She hung the apron behind the door, and Mrs Jane sighed.

'No. You never *lied* to me. That you didn't. Never you tell a lie, children,' she said, wagging a finger at us kindly, but you could see she was still sad-looking. 'Nothing is worse than a lie. You tell a lie and it'll be round the world before the truth has got its boots on,' and she turned the gas off under the kettle.

But no one was interested in my voles. So I just shut up.

Our father was sitting on a little camp-stool in the long grass, with his travelling easel and his paintbox beside him. I was allowed to sit near him, but a bit behind him, not in the 'eye line', because he said I fidgeted about and it put him off. So I sat very still, watching. And it was a quite good painting of the view down to the Daukeses' cottage, with trees and grass and everything, and in the distance the humpy shape of Windover Hill. I mean, you could easily see that and know where it was, and then, when he was washing out a brush in the jam-jar of turps, and wiping it on a piece of old curtain, I asked him if it had been very nice in Germany when they were there, and he said no, not very. When I asked him if he had bought the machine-things for *The Times*, he said no, too expensive, but another English paper had bought them instead. You could tell he was pretty fed up that *The Times* was not rich enough, but all he said was did I like the things our mother had bought in Germany, and so of course I said yes. What else do you say? I got three quite funny corks with carved people's heads on top. They were to stopper

our Tizer, she said. Only we never left enough Tizer to
stopper. One of the faces was a chimney-sweep, with a
top hat and a black face, another was a fat lady with a
bosom and long blond plaits, and the last one was of a
dreadful old man with a red nose and a mouth laughing
with no teeth. They were all laughing, and they all had
red noses and I thought they were pretty daft, but our
mother had thought they would be 'amusing'. So we said
that they were. My sister got a very nice little box with a
huge church painted on it, and when you opened the lid it
played a tinkling tune which our father said was the
German National Anthem and wasn't really suitable. It
was pretty gloomy, but didn't go on for long. And they
brought Lally a record for her 'collection' and there was
something called 'I'm One of the Nuts from Barcelona' on
one side and '*Trink, Trink, Trink, Brüder Trink!*' which
was pretty silly, and anyway we couldn't understand it.
But she also got a nice little doll, all made of pine cones
and feathers, which was quite interesting. If you liked little
dolls. Which I didn't. But Lally made a lot of enjoying
sounds, so I suppose that she did.

I asked him if Germany was very far away and he said
not far enough, and that I was a lucky boy not to live
there and to live instead where I did. I said I knew that,
and I jolly well did. Nowhere was better than the cottage
and Great Meadow, and just as he was mixing up some
greenish paint I asked him how he painted the sky. And he
said he couldn't paint skies, they were very difficult, and
so he was going to paint a tree and would I please shut up
and go and see what sort of trees there were in the hedge
just below us. Which was silly really, because he could

easily see for himself. But he told me to go off and bring him back a leaf from every tree and bush I could find. A different leaf! I said it would take ages and ages, and he said that is exactly what he hoped, and when I had got them all I could have a penny for something scrumptious, he said, at Baker's. So I went off.

Anyway, it was very nice to have them back again. Our mother was pretty and funny, and she and Lally were talking and laughing up in the vegetable garden. I could hear them clear as clear, and our mother said it was wonderful to be back in England again, and how were the aphids and thrips this year? And Lally said she didn't rightly know, and they laughed and I heard my mother beginning her 'Silly Song'. Anyway, that's what my sister and I called it because she used to sing it whenever our father was somewhere near. It was called 'Always', and we thought it a bit disgusting, because sometimes we would see them walking up the path from the O.M., arm in arm, and she'd be just singing this daft song. It made me feel really a bit embarrassed. But then I suppose they didn't know we were watching.

Clambering about in the hedge for the leaves for our father, I could hear her plain as plain. She was hanging out some things on the clothes-line in her gypsy-sort-of dress, and Lally and my sister were looking for one lettuce which hadn't bolted, and my mother was singing away, 'I'll be loving youoooo . . . always . . . With a love that's trueoo . . . always . . .' But it did feel really pretty good having them back. They had liked my voles very much indeed, and my father told me that the river bank in the box was made of paper machey. And when I asked him what that was he just said to ask him tomorrow. But he really was *most* interested. So that was all right.

You could hear the rattle and clatter of the reaper right up the path, and when we got to the end of the lane and crossed the chalk road everyone was there and had bagged the best places in the shade. It was terrifically hot, even so early in the morning. Well, early for us. I'd heard the distant clattering through my bedroom window, and the sun was already up, so we were a bit late, but Lally had said what's the hurry then, I haven't got your basket ready, and eat your Bemax, and so on. So we did. And all the time they were all down in the field called Long Bottom, which was quite rude except it was the big field at the foot of Windover. We walked along the hedge under the elms and found a place where no one else was. People put their bags and baskets and the bottles of cold tea to keep cool in the shade, so we knew not to intrude, because even if we did live 'up at the Rectory' we were still Foreigners, even after all those years. Well, quite a lot. Five or six, about.

So we put our basket under a big ash tree down at the bottom, and my sister just had a look to see if the wet cloth round the ginger beer bottle was still wet, and then we went out into the very edge of the field, where the reaper had already cut, and where everyone was busy gleaning – Winnie Moss and Beattie Fluke and Mrs Daukes. All round the edges of the corn, where it had been cleared, the men stood here and there quietly each chewing a bit of straw, their rifles sort of drooping over their left arms, but really ready to swing up and bang off at a rabbit. The

The Gleaning.

rabbits and mice and things all ran into the middle, and Winnie Moss, who waved at us and came to have a 'cool down' in the shade, said that they did think some old fox had run bang-slap into the centre, and they were all waiting for the reaper to trim it all down.

It was quite nice walking along in the stubble because I was wearing my old Wellingtons and no socks, and my sister was a bit daft and she was wearing her sandals without socks, so pretty soon she got all cut and scratched around the ankles, because the new-cut stubble was sharp as a razor. But I didn't bother to say anything, even when I saw the blood and the scratches. We just went on gleaning away, although where we were gleaning was where all the others had been gleaning before we got there. So it wasn't much, just the stalks here and there. But Lally had said don't intrude, and so we didn't. Winnie Moss said she had already gleaned enough corn for a 'best brown' and she'd have to be there for a month of Sundays before she had enough gleaned to make half a dozen loaves. I said well, why was she doing it now, and she said what a silly question. It was the 'old way', and the old way was going, and anyway, who would glean the stuff left over? What with corn so expensive she reckoned to bag a sack by evening for her chickens, so I said that we hadn't got any chickens and so she could have what we gleaned, and she said that was really kind of us.

And then Miss Aleford came galumphing along in a straw hat and gaiters, and said we were welcome to join in. It was her field, so I suppose she was being polite. Then she said no more capers with harvest mice this year! I was a bit surprised that she had remembered stamping on one

of mine last year and squashing it flat, but I didn't say
anything. I just laughed. Well, you do when people say
difficult things, and I wasn't going to tell her about my
voles. I didn't care about harvest mice after Sat and Sun
had gone. Dead and gone, Lally had said, so that was that.

My father had told me that it was very difficult to paint
a sky, but he would have had a wonderful time down in
Long Bottom because all around us were the Downs, at
the back the hedge and the elms and ash trees, in the
middle just the golden corn square, getting a bit smaller all
the time with the old reaper chugging round and round,
and high above (well, where else would it be?) was the
sky. Just blue. Blue as blue. No clouds, not even a bird,
nothing. Sparkling blue for ever. And hot.

Beattie Fluke had settled herself down in a clump of
dock leaves and tall grasses and was fanning herself with
her beret. She laughed to us, and that was proof that she
really hadn't got any teeth at all, and our father was right
when he said that 'all her intake was liquid'. Which I
didn't really understand, but seeing the no-teeth part now
I think that he actually meant that she couldn't chew
things. Only drink things. It was a bit worrying, because
she was jolly fat, but very nice really, and she had a face
exactly like the stoppers our mother had brought from
Germany. All laughing and red.

'What you got in your ditty-bag, then?' she called. I
said I didn't really know what a 'ditty-bag' was and so she
told me, and said it was clear as clear I wasn't a sailor-boy,
and laughed like anything. So I said only ginger beer, and
she said leave out the ginger and she'd be happy. So it was
all a bit of a worry, and then I went down the field and

began gleaning with my sister, who had quite a huge sheaf which we carried up, with mine later, to Mrs Moss.

All you could hear down in the middle of the big field was the rattle of the reaper and the distant talking of women, or children laughing and, now and then, the crack of a rifle when one of the men took a shot at a rabbit. And then, when it really seemed to be terribly hot, the reaper stopped with a clanking and shudder, and a huff of smoke wandered into the blue, and the men jumped off, and everyone came back up the field, past the two big horses swishing their tails by the pink and blue waggon standing in the shade. Everyone settled down under the trees among the campion and ox-eye daisies, while the women opened bottles and unpacked the food and called to the children.

We sat up in our part under the ash tree and my sister took off her sandals and her feet were all cut and bloody. Serve her right. But there was ginger beer and cold pigeon pie, a chunk of Double Gloucester and slices of apple tart. It was really quite decent. Except for the flies and the wasps. The men were all lying in the grass with their arms across their eyes, and they had strings tied round their trouser legs to stop the rats and mice from running up their legs, and that suddenly reminded me of Sat and Sun and, even though I was very happy among all the people and under the huge blue sky which you could just see through the leaves of the ash tree, I felt a little bit miserable. But then Len Diplock from the Court came past with a pole over his shoulder and six rabbits hanging by their crossed legs, and he offered them to Winnie Moss, fourpence each, and to Beattie Fluke, who was sitting with

Mrs Daukes and another lady, and they all screamed with laughter and said who did he think they were? Gordon Selfridge or the Prince of Wales? And they wouldn't have one, not if he made them a ha'penny! 'Vermin!' said Beattie Fluke. 'Vermin that's what, nice in a stew, good in a bake, but not at fourpence, what with a pint of beer more than a penny!'

So he went off, laughing, and everyone was very happy and starting to clear up their rubbish. Then we heard the pop and patter of the reaper starting up again. Long Bottom had to be finished before the light went and they couldn't see properly to pick off the rabbits and the old fox, if he was in the middle. Mrs Daukes said not only was there a fox in there but Mr Daukes had put up two hare, and they were sitting just waiting until there was no more corn left to cut. My sister started moaning about how cruel it was, but Winnie Moss just said, 'That's nature, my dear. It's the country way. Don't have no London manners down here. Life isn't all ice cream and satin cushions. If there's a fox in there they'll get 'im. Or he'll get our hens and then what? Just bite their heads off for the spite of it. I seen 'em bite the legs off all Mrs Witts's whole flock!' And she called across to the lady sitting with Mrs Fluke and Mrs Daukes we didn't know. 'True as I'm here, Meg, correct? Your hens? That old fox. Got 'em all by their legs?'

'True! Twelve Leghorns, lovely they was. Just bit his way up into their shed and grabbed them by their legs. Didn't touch the bodies, just legs. 'Orrid it was. You never did see such a sight, all alive and no legs!'

And Winnie Moss looked at my sister with a quite kind

smile. 'See? Not a lie. Wicked they are. Don't you have no pity for them rats and foxes, real wicked.'

So that shut her up a bit, and I was just starting to put the stopper on the ginger beer bottle when Miss Aleford called out, quite rudely I thought, 'Boy! You there! Look what we found. I have a feeling it could belong to you, you seem to have a mouse fixation.'

And she had something cupped in her hands, and was walking quite slowly, and there were two men behind her. I got up and she opened her hands carefully. 'White. A white mouse. I reckon it might be yours? What do you think, eh?'

And it was Sun. Lying in her hands, wheezing away, his tail all draggly. But he was enormous, much bigger than he had been, so I said I think it might be one of my mice, maybe Sun who was white but he was smaller. And Miss Aleford said, 'It's no "he", it's a "she", and I very much fear it's going to have babies, look!' And she gently turned him over and all his underneath was pink, with little red teats, so it was a girl-mouse. And I said yes! it is Sun, and Miss Aleford said that George here had found it under a stook, and she very much feared it was all too late and that it would die of fright if it didn't die of something else, and the George-person said he'd found it in a ball of hay when he was stacking the stooks.

'The poor thing, it is the fright!' said Miss Aleford. 'It's got to have warmth and darkness.' And then she unbuttoned her blouse and pushed her fist into her bosom, which was a bit surprising, but we didn't say anything because it was her farm and her field and her harvest. And then she took it out again and shook her head slowly, and said,

'No. No hope. I fear it's passed away, poor little thing. You'd better take it off and give it a respectful burial. Probably mated with a wild one. It was *doomed*.'

She gave me Sun in her cupped hand, and I took him and it was quite certain he was dead, with his little pink feet crossed and a droplet of blood on his nose. I felt really mouldy. But my sister helped me to scrape out a hole in the roots of the big ash tree, and we buried him there . . . I mean her.

And then there was a terrific sound of guns cracking, and shouts that the rabbits were running. Some of the boys (I saw Reg and Perce tearing around) had big sticks to club them or the hares and my sister said she didn't like this part, even if it *was* nature's way and she'd rather have ice cream and satin cushions or whatever it was.

So she collected our basket and things and wandered on up to the cottage, but I stayed on and gleaned quite a lot and gave our big sheaf to Winnie Moss to add to hers. The square in the middle of the field was getting smaller and smaller, and the reaper went round and round, shaking and clattering. The men stood about with their guns in their hands and not lying across their forearms now because it was getting close to the end and the fox had to run. But I didn't really want to wait. With poor Sun dead, and full of babies, I thought I'd just go home, because everyone was getting excited and laughing and running about and Beattie Fluke called out that this was the best part of the day, but I didn't think so. So I turned and went up the lane home.

After supper I went out into the front garden and stood

between the rows of carrots and beetroot, listening to the shots from Long Bottom. It was still quite light. We hadn't even lit the lamps yet. The sky was a lovely faded colour, the bats were wheeling about in the still air and right behind the cottage, miles away beyond Firle Beacon even, a huge pale yellow moon was rising and Lally said it was the harvest moon and emptied her dust pan and all the supper crumbs into the larkspur.

And down the lane, going towards Court Farm and Litlington, we could hear the big waggon creaking and crunching. There were laughter and shouts and then some of the ladies started singing 'Ramona' together, and we just stood and listened to them until they drifted quite away.

And it was all still again.

Chapter 8

I had a funny sort of feeling that something quite curious was happening when it was our mother, and not Lally, who opened the curtains in my bedroom and told me to get up and get dressed quickly. She was wearing her long floaty dressing-gown with feathery stuff down the front, and her boudoir cap, all covered in little rosebuds. She never walked about the house dressed like that. And she had no make-up on, and she looked very worried.

'I'll go and wake your sister. Lally's not at all well.' She went away, and I felt pretty frightened. I had never heard of Lally being 'not at all well' in my life before, so I got up and dressed and went down to the bathroom to clean my teeth, but I didn't bother about washing the back of my neck and so on because no one had told me to and I forgot. My sister came in in her liberty bodice and bloomers, which was a bit peculiar because usually she wouldn't even let me see her rotten old knickers, even though I didn't really care anyway. She squeezed out some Euthymol on her brush and we spat and rinsed together and the water was running, and everything suddenly seemed unhappy and funny.

'I wonder what's wrong with her. Lally, I mean?'

I combed my hair with water and saw a bit of a spot at the side of my nose. 'She had a headache last night. Remember? And we didn't play anything after our homework. Remember? She said she felt "peaky". It's very frightening. If she's ill, I mean.'

My sister poked the tube of toothpaste at me. 'You are really *vile*. You've squashed it in the middle again, it's all bulgy.'

I told her I was worried so I had forgotten and then we heard our mother calling up from the hall that she had telephoned Dr Henderson and she'd be coming as soon as possible.

'Oh dear!' said my sister. 'The doctor! How really terrible! It must be bad.'

Then our mother came in and told us to hurry up. She had a cup of tea in her hand and was taking it along the corridor to Lally's room, which had a very shut door. 'Go downstairs to the morning room, the kettle's boiling. I'll be down in a minute.'

And my sister wailed and said she had to get her gymslip on, so our mother called out, 'Go and do it, and *you*' – she meant me – 'put on your tie.' Then she went into Lally's room and shut the door gently.

It was a bit peculiar. Our mother was being just as bossy as Lally, and she sounded very different from her usual voice ... busy-sounding. Normally we used to get up, dress and wash, and Lally would be checking that things were aired or ironed or had clean collars. Then we'd go down to breakfast and have tea and eggs and bacon, and toast or something, and the foul Bemax or Virol. It would be all normal and comfortable and 'have you got your exercise books, pencil box, geography book and the penny for the poor orphan children in Africa?' That was for my sister, who went to the convent, not to my school, and I reckon that those nuns must have sent simply hundreds of poor African orphans up the cardboard

ladder to heaven. I mean, every time you put a penny in
the orphan box, one of the nuns would shove your paper-
cut-out orphan up another rung of the ladder. Our father
said it was a terrible 'con trick', which we didn't understand, but he said it nicely, and was laughing when he said
it, so it didn't seem serious, especially when he said that St
Martha's and St Ursula's must have saved entire tribes
between them. That made it feel really 'worth while', as
Lally said.

After all that we had to go up to the lav to 'have a try',
then wash our hands and go up to our parents' room,
knock on the door, and when someone said 'Come in' we
went in to say 'Good morning'. Usually our father was in
his bathroom, shaving, and our mother was sitting at a
little table in the bay window with her tea and the *Daily
Sketch*, which was 'suitable' for ladies and quite small to
hold to read. It was all very comfortable and safe.

But today didn't feel safe at all and our father was
sitting in the morning room, which was most unusual
except on Saturdays, reading his *Times* and eating a piece
of toast. He said that he had made some tea and if we
needed more water there was plenty in the kettle and we'd
have to wait for our mother to come down to feed us
because he just didn't know what we ate and anyway
hadn't the time. Then he rustled away at the paper and
my sister said, 'We normally have eggs and bacon, or a
sausage, and toast and marmalade'. And he just said, not
lowering the paper at all, 'Do you now?' Which was a bit
rude and dismissy really. Anyway, our mother came into
the room and said to sit down and she'd get us some
breakfast and then she told our father that Lally was quite

wretched, but that Henderson was coming over as soon as she could.

It was a pretty rotten breakfast, while our father was reading and chewing his toast with terrible crunching sounds. Lally would have given him a rap on the knuckles for that, but our mother was too busy burning the bacon, and the eggs were all sort of brown and frilly round the edges and her feathery sleeves kept catching on the frying-pan handle. She was pretty cross, you could tell easily.

So we just sat still and didn't say anything, except my sister, who said could we go up and see Lally before we went to school? Our father put down his paper and said as soon as the doctor came, but not before, and just at that moment the bell rang and my mother rushed out of the kitchen and the frying-pan fell on the floor, but it was only hot fat (we had the eggs and the bacon on our plates), so our father picked it up and said there was less panic in all of Printing House Square, which is where he worked. Then our mother came back and said that Dr Henderson was better left alone, and she'd speak to her when she came down and what had happened to the frying-pan? And our father told her she had knocked it down. And you could tell that they were both pretty fed up.

When Dr Henderson banged on the door and came in she was very nice to my sister and me, and smiled and arranged her tie. She and my mother went into the hall to have a private sort of talk. Our father folded his paper and said he must be off, so we sat there in the empty morning room with a terrible smell of burning bacon everywhere, which would never have been allowed if Lally had been there. Only she wasn't.

'You can go and see her, just for a moment, but no kisses, and *don't* go into her room. We don't know if it's flu or something, so just put your heads round the door and remember she's very tired. Don't fuss her. The doctor is coming again this afternoon. To keep an eye on her. Off you go.'

So we did, except that I got my Vim tin which I was starting the save-up-for-Christmas business with, and I tried to shake out some coppers, but it was quite difficult because the 'tin' was really only made of cardboard, and just the top and the bottom were the tin parts, and I had cut a slit in the side to put in the pennies and pieces that people gave me when I asked. (My father said I was begging, but I really wasn't, I was just asking, for a penny or two. If I was really lucky it was a threepenny bit, and once I got a whole sixpence, by mistake. But too late. It slid into the slot and it was all for Christmas presents, not daft orphans.)

So I had to break the whole tin to open it, because the cardboard was all twirly and tight, and I couldn't get the money out through the slit even with a knife blade. There was quite a lot spilled on the table: one sixpence and three threepenny bits and a lot of coppers. My sister said, 'What are you doing? Supposing we get the burglars in? Then what? You'll lose everything.' I told her not to be so silly and she said *I* was silly: no one would think of looking in a rotten old Vim tin for money, so what would I do now? I said I'd hide it all in Jesus on the altar in my bedroom, because he was quite hollow all the way up and no one would dream of stealing anything from Jesus. But my sister said that they would, once they saw that he had yellow hair and a black beard, and that when I had painted him I had got him all muddled. I said M.Y.O.B. and took a sixpence and some coppers out of the money which I hid inside Him, and asked Him to keep an eye on it while I was at school.

It was quite a lot really after I'd taken out the sixpence. About two shillings in pennies and halfpennies and the threepenny bits. I was jolly pleased, because it was only March, so goodness knows how rich I'd be by December for the presents. It would be quite easy: I'd just keep it all in Jesus and then put it in another Vim tin when there was an empty one. Anyway, we went off to school.

Our mother was busy in the kitchen doing her eyelashes in her compact-mirror, with a very squinty face. She said, be careful, and mind about the roads, and that she hated being seen by people so early in the morning without 'her face' on, and not to kiss her because she had just done her lipstick. So we just went off, and coming back from school that afternoon I went into the chemist's on Heath Street and bought a titchy little bottle, green glass and quite flat, like a pocket watch. It had an old-fashioned lady with a basket on it and it was called 'Essence of Devon Violets'. The lady behind the counter said it was just the 'trick' for the sick-room, refreshing and 'dainty'. It cost sixpence or a bit more, but it was better than that old Cologne stuff Winnie Moss was so braggy about. Lally could put it on her handkerchief and then rub it on her forehead. If it was hot. Which, our mother said, it was. She was running a very high fever and the doctor would be here immediately, so to go up, not to go too near, and give her the Devon Violets. But that was all, because she was very miserable.

Her room was stuffy, and she looked sad and flat-looking lying in her little bed, all rumpled and sweaty. Her hair was shiny wet on her head, and it was so thin you could see the pink parts of her showing, and she was wearing a pair of our father's pyjamas because she had soaked all her nightdresses she said, and not to come too near because she feared she had flu or something. I put the Devon Violets on her bedside table and said that the smell would cheer her up, and she whispered that I was a dear boy, and to look after my sister and she'd be right as rain tomorrow. A good night's rest was all she needed, and when was the doctor coming? Then my sister pushed round the door, and said she missed her, or something silly, and Lally waved us away and said to close the door and go and help our mother. So we did. My sister said, going down the stairs so that Lally couldn't possibly hear, 'I think she's got a dreadful germ from all those terrible people she sits with at the pictures on Sunday! She goes every Sunday, on her day off. Sometimes she goes simply miles away, to Golders Green! To the Ionic, sometimes to the Lido. Once she even went as far as awful Camden Town to see a flick. It's very dangerous and I think it's God's curse.'

I said don't be so daft, hundreds of people go to the pictures on Sunday, only, *we* aren't allowed. Lally loves them and tells us all the stories, and my sister said she was sick to death of the stories but hoped she hadn't brought back something ghastly from all those awful people, because only wicked people broke the law. Our father had said so. And the African orphans sometimes had leprosy, and their arms and feet fell off and terrible things happened to them, the nuns said, because they lived in Idleness and Ignorance, and that's what going to the pictures on Sunday was.

I didn't argue, it was useless. She just went on down into the hall at the exact moment that Dr Henderson arrived looking a bit flustered in her man's suit, with her black bag and her tie all fluttering.

'Have you been up to Miss Jane's room? I trust not?' she said rather crossly, and I said we had only put our heads round the door and I'd given her a present, but no touching. She just pushed past rather rudely and told me to call our mother, who was at the top of the stairs anyway, looking very pretty, in a very nice frock with buttons down the front, with her eyelashes 'mascara-ed' and her hair all combed and tidy.

They went off along the corridor to Lally's room, while we wandered into the morning room and wondered who would make the tea. My sister said we could lay the table and that would make it feel a bit more like nearly-time-for-tea. So we put down the cups and saucers and I said that I thought that Lally had liked the Devon Violets, and my sister said it was a very nice thing to do, which made me feel quite cheerful. I felt even better when we found there was half a Fuller's Walnut in the cake tin. And a *whole* jar of fish paste, anchovy, unopened, so there would be plenty for us both, because I knew that my mother detested fish paste and poor Lally was much too ill anyway to eat a thing. Then we heard voices and Dr Henderson came in with our mother. They were a bit funny looking, which was quite frightening, and Dr Henderson said we weren't to go up to Miss Jane again and then, the worst part, she said, 'Margaret, I think you should try to get the children away if you can. Any chance of getting them down to the cottage? Fresh air? It would be wise.'

And my mother looked at us and said, 'Lally is *very* ill indeed. She has scarlet fever, and it is very infectious. So things are going to be rather difficult. You'll have to understand that, and try and help me.'

Dr Henderson said she knew we would, and that she would call the ambulance now, and did Miss Jane have relations? She'd get on to the fumigation people and call the isolation hospital, and then she and our mother hurried out into the hall. And my sister burst into tears. Well, she would, I suppose. It was very frightening and there were a lot of words we hadn't heard before.

We could hear them telephoning in the hall. I put my arms round my sister and told her to shut up (but nicely) because she was making too much noise and I couldn't hear what they were saying on the telephone. So she did shut up a bit, just sniffing and moaning, quietly, while I listened at the door, but all I could hear was the doctor telling our address and saying 'the patient', which I knew must mean poor Lally. So suddenly she was something else. Not Miss Jane or Lally. A 'patient'. My mother said she'd have to send a telegram to Mrs Jane, and she hurried back into the morning room and told us to have a glass of milk and cake, or something, because she really hadn't time to do it herself.

There was a lot of telephoning that day, I can tell you, and in the end we were sent away to stay with my sister's very best friend at the convent, Giovanna Govoni, who lived in a house with a huge chestnut tree quite near. Her mother, Aunt Isali (not kith and kin, of course, but very nice indeed), said that we had to keep 'out of the way' at our house because there were lots of things happening. She didn't say *what* lots of things. But it didn't matter because her house was simply lovely. It was so full of terrific things and smells of cooking. And, another good mark, they had a huge glass bowl of big goldfish just swimming around, and one was white and you could see all its insides quite clearly. I found that very interesting.

When we were all sitting at the table in their kitchen having supper, Aunt Isali showed me how to sprinkle some rather salty cheese, which she had just grated, over my spaghetti. Then she told us all that Lally had been taken to Dollis Hill Isolation Hospital, and that sounded pretty frightening because she had gone off in an ambulance! I thought it was a bit rotten not to have actually seen an ambulance, I mean not close to, but what was *really* awful was that she said that our whole house had to be 'fumigated', which meant disinfected. Like with Jeyes and the pink carbolic in the privy. But worse. So scarlet fever must be pretty terrible, so poor Lally. And all because she went to the pictures on Sundays! Aunt Isali said you could catch it anywhere, so not to speak in such a silly manner. So I shut up.

But it really was pretty decent being with the Govonis, with Giovanna and her baby brothers, Italo and Mario, and, best of all, her grandmother, who was called Madame Chiese and couldn't speak any English but smiled at us all the same and fed ant's eggs to the goldfish and made something with a crochet hook when she couldn't talk to us. It was really lovely being with them, and the smells

and the voices were all funny, just like being abroad.
Really nice if you had *them*, and not fumigation and everything. It was a bit annoying that I did not see the ambulance or the fumigation van, which was a pretty bad mark,
but Aunt Isali said we were better out of the way, and that
our mother was getting everything packed up to go down
to the cottage tomorrow. That was pretty amazing because
although it was a weekend, in the middle of term, we
usually had to stay in Hampstead for the exams. Worse
luck.

Then she said we both had to be very kind to our
mother because she had had a tremendous amount to do
and had had a dreadful shock when she went to the isolation hospital in a taxi and they said that there was no such
person as a Miss E. Jane listed. Our mother had made a
terrific fuss and said she had seen it all happen with her
own eyes, and they were all very huffy and rude, but then
they found that they *had* made a terrible mistake, because
there was a *Mister* E. Jane in the men's ward, so they
apologized. It was on account of our father's pyjamas and
the awful boy's hair cut, and of course our mother was
furious, and she had had a most dreadful fright, but so had
the isolation hospital. When that was sorted out she came
back to telephone Aunt Isali and say we were all going
away, into the fresh air.

So the next morning we got into the O.M., and I wore
my new blue suit from Daniel Neal's, my very first long
trousers and only to be worn for absolute Best, not at
school or anything silly. But they were all in such a
muddle, I mean the grown-ups, that they didn't even
notice, and the house smelled simply terrible and dead,

and it took me ages to get struggling Minnehaha into his travelling cage, and then we had to put in the cases and food and his cage, so no one even looked at my new suit from Daniel Neal's, or even asked about it. Which was very good. But I heard our father say thank god this is a normal Saturday because tomorrow he could be back in peace and quiet at Printing House Square with his paper, and our mother said that paper meant more to him than his own family, and he said yes, sometimes it does. Especially with Monday coming up. Which I didn't understand but I could see they were pretty cross with each other. But they hadn't seen my suit. So that was all right.

Then our father buttoned us under the black tonneau-cover, and fixed the big windscreen across the top, between the driving-seats and us, so we'd not be blown away (he drove terribly fast), and then all we could see of our parents were their helmets and the scarves flying and our mother's angry face in her driving-mirror. They were having a bit of a row, but my sister said if we can't *hear* it we don't really know that they are, they just *look* furious. So that was sensible. I thought.

It was very exciting driving so fast, with the wind roaring past us, and we couldn't even hear Minnehaha howling away in his cage beside our feet under the tonneau. We couldn't hear, but we *knew* that he did that, because he hated the cage-basket and hated being in the dark. So. But we got to the halfway stop at the Felbridge Arms for a packet of crisps and some American ice cream soda, and our parents went into the bar. They seemed a bit more cheerful, because our father actually put his arm round her waist, which was pretty soppy, but perhaps they'd be in a better mood later. I let Minnehaha out for a breath of fresh air while we drank our soda.

This was what we always did driving to the cottage. He was on a little collar and lead, and he would sit, quite happily, on the top of the rolled-up cover of the O.M., just sniffing and looking around, and I was telling him that I'd take him to do a pee when there was a terrible roaring noise and a motorbike and sidecar came tearing along, rushing past honking its horn, and sending dust and dead leaves high into the air. Then it roared away and so did Minnehaha, pulling the lead out of my hand and skipping and hopping off into the dead bracken by the car park. My sister screamed (a fat lot of good that did) and I shouted (and that didn't do much more). Our parents came out of the pub and our mother said, 'And *now* what do we do?' Our father said, 'It's that bloody cat!' (which was really ghastly), but he asked the people in the bar to have a look for a large tabby with a little collar, and we were allowed half an hour to go and find him. Although we called and hollered, and even asked people in the lane, we never saw a sight of him. But the quite nice man behind the bar said he'd keep a look-out, and took my father's address. But we never saw Minnehaha again. Not ever.

So that was a pretty awful way to get to the cottage, and what was almost as bad was that Mrs Daukes was in her garden burning rubbish, and she said she didn't know we'd be down this weekend, nothing had been done, there had been no message, and she was sorry she was sure. Our father just bit his lip and made us carry the baggage up the track. There was no fire laid, no water in the buckets, and it smelled of damp and dark, and it was very miserable.

Just like us. But then our mother lit one of the lamps, and I had to go and get some water from the pump, and my sister looked for the hot water bottles. Our father arrived with Minnehaha's empty cage and just said, 'Do you think this is perhaps the end of the world?' And our mother said perhaps it was, but not before tomorrow. So that made me cheer up a bit. And no one had said a thing about my suit. So that was all right. Almost.

Our father made a huge fire in their sitting-room, which was rather nice, because he liked making fires. He even made them on our picnics in the summer when we had Thermos flasks, so we didn't even need them. But our mother said if he enjoyed it let him do it. And it was very welcome in the cottage and most especially in their room.

I had to go and pump up hundreds of buckets of water, well, quite a lot anyway, and carry them up to the lean-to, so of course I had to change my jacket from Daniel Neals and put on a holey old cardigan, but no one seemed to notice my trousers. Good luck.

Our mother worked the old Primus stoves and we all began to settle down, except it was awful with no Minnehaha anywhere, but I didn't say anything because it would make us all too miserable.

In the evening, when it was getting dark, our parents had to drive down to the village to telephone *The Times*, as usual, just to check in, and our mother asked us to do the vegetables for her, onions and potatoes, because we were to have liver and bacon and mashed for supper. So that was pretty good. And she said to behave ourselves and not 'go rushing about' and they'd only be an hour. So we did the vegetables, and then we laid the table in their

the Sitting room –

room, which was very pretty with the hanging lamp burning, and the big fire in the open hearth, and the lamps everywhere, and the table looking jolly nice with the blue Spode china and a jam-jar of daffodils my sister had picked in the long grass by the lean-to. It was all really quite good. I had put on our father's painting-smock, the one old Mr Dick had given him, so that I didn't muck up my new trousers, and I tied it round the waist, because it was too big for me, with a piece of binder-twine I found. I was just shoving a big apple-log on to the fire when there was a sort of loud 'Poff!' and my sister screamed that I was on fire. The back of the smock had caught in the iron basket which was blazing away, and so was I. It was all behind me, and I couldn't get the binder-twine off. I kept tugging, but no luck, and my sister kept screaming standing in the doorway. There was a rug on the brick floor, but I couldn't grab it because it would have knocked over a little table and an oil lamp. The flames were really roaring away, so I just pushed my sister, so she fell over, and then rushed through the hall into the lean-to where the buckets of water which I had pumped that afternoon were. It was a bit lucky really, because with all the draught the smock was blazing.

It was pretty awful. There was water all over the floor, and I had upset two buckets. There was a dreadful smell of burning, but the fire was out and I got a knife and cut the wretched twine. When I started to try and take off the smock all the right sleeve had burned away, and the cardie sleeve was all melted and black, so I hid the smock in the empty range in the kitchen and pulled off the cardigan. My arm was starting to get all red and funny-looking, but I put on an old school blazer, so no one would see, and then we mopped up the water and everything, and my sister was just sobbing quietly because she had had such a fright (and so had I). I told her she must say nothing about what happened when the parents got back, and if they asked about the water we would just say I had upset a bucket. So that was easy. But we had to open the doors to get the smell of burning out, and I hid the burned cardie up in the elder bush by the privy.

So we were quite all right when our parents came in looking quite happy and laughing. Except when our mother sniffed hard and said, 'I only asked you to do the vegetables! You haven't been doing anything quite silly?' And we said no, but my arm was beginning to hurt rather a lot, and then our mother said, 'Now what *has* happened? You've singed off all your eyelashes. You had wonderful eyelashes! Just like mine . . . What *have* you been doing?'

And my sister suddenly said I'd caught fire and it was terrible. So everything got found out. Our father told me to take off my blazer, but I couldn't because my arm had sort of swelled up and filled the sleeve. Then he said, rather loudly, 'Margaret, get me some scissors, quickly.' He cut all the sleeve of the old blazer and peeled the cloth away and my arm looked like a huge grey sausage. It was just one terrific blister – my shirt sleeve had burned right off – and it was beginning to throb like anything all the way from my elbow to my fingertips and the palm of my hand looked dreadful and fat and full of water.

'Oh god!' said our mother. 'What has he done, Ulric?'

Of course, she only said that because she was so shocked (she could see perfectly clearly), and so was I, but our father just got a towel and said, 'It's pretty bad. I'll get him down to the village to Wilmott.' He wrapped my arm, very gently indeed, in the towel and carried me – well, I was really half leaning on him – down the track to the O.M. He was very decent in the car. He never asked me what had happened, or about my long trousers, or anything.

We parked in Waterloo Square, by the Market Cross, and walked up to Dr Wilmott's house and rang and rang. After ages a grumpy woman came and said Dr Wilmott was playing bridge over at Alciston and it was his 'night off' anyway. There was another doctor who had just moved in, *but* She was a Woman.

So we went to her house. It was all dark, and I was half lying, half standing against our father, and he was knocking and knocking, and it was very dark and terribly cold. Suddenly there was a light in an upstairs window, and a woman's face peered out, and our father shouted it was very serious, so she opened the window but said she couldn't treat anyone because she was ill herself. With scarlet fever. Our father said I had very bad burns and please would she help. So she shut the window, the room went dark, and my father said, 'Don't worry, she's coming down. There's a light on now in the hall.'

Then we were inside, and it was a little hall-place, with a big wooden chest against a wall. The lady doctor had straggly hair and a fawn dressing-gown, and I heard her make a sort of breathy noise when she saw my arm. She told our father that all she had in the house was a pair of nail-scissors, and that she was probably infectious. Would he take the risk? He said, 'Yes. Please go ahead.' So I sat with him on the wooden chest, and she got the nail scissors and a bottle of something blue. It smelled awful as she poured it in a saucer and put the scissors in. Then she cut all the huge, shiny blisters up my arm and my hand, and said that I had to be got to a hospital and properly dressed. (Except for my burned shirt, I *was* dressed. *And* with long trousers on.) But she just said that I could possibly have second-degree burns, whatever that was, and to get me into 'proper hands' as soon as possible. She bandaged me up, and made a kind of sling, and I didn't blub. So that anyone could see, anyway.

There were pills to take when I got back to the cottage, to make me sleep. It was all pretty awful, and I hurt like anything. But I didn't say so. She was very nice, and said she'd just come to the village and hoped to be able to practise, but Dr Wilmott was against her, and so were many of his older patients. Our father said he'd never be able to thank her enough, and he'd settle her bill as soon as he could, and before she shut the door she called, 'Good luck! Jolly brave, you were!' Which made me feel quite good. But it didn't stop the hurting.

In my Hampstead bedroom, with the bluetits on the wallpaper, Dr Henderson was jolly bossy indeed with our mother. I just lay in my bed with my eyes closed to pretend not to listen. But, of course, I did. Even though I was hurting like anything.

'Margaret, you can't possibly nurse him here. The hospital has all the things he'll need, equipment.'

'No. Absolutely no. He's mine and he stays here. I can cope.'

'That arm has to be bathed three, or four, times a day, in water as hot as he can possibly bear.'

'I know that. You have told me already. We have been doing that.'

'How can you manage? Possibly? What will you bathe it in, elbow to fingertips?'

'My fish kettle. If it'll take a salmon-grilse, it'll take my son's forearm. He's not leaving this house. He stays. His sister has a raging temperature, and you aren't "sure" as you say. Well, if she *has* to go to the isolation place, if it *is* that, he stays here. I have had enough disaster, no more.'

I quite liked that our mother had said 'mine', but then Dr Henderson said, quietly, 'Disaster? Margaret, thank your god on your knees this moment that you are not Mrs Lindbergh!'

And our mother's voice was very cross indeed, and she said, 'No, but I *am* Mrs van den Bogaerde, and that is all I care about at the moment.'

There was a bit of a silence, so I opened my eyes a squint and saw Dr Henderson packing things into her bag, and then she said, 'I'll go and see your daughter. If she has contracted the thing, he's almost certain to get it too, with that raw wound. Face up to it, Margaret.'

Then she went away and it was a bit quiet. I saw, through slitty eyes, my mother going to the little window over the garden, and she said aloud that she would face it. If, and when, it all happened. Which was jolly brave of her, because, the night before, when we got back from the cottage, my sister said she was hot and had a sore throat, and that was very worrying. But if she *did* have scarlet fever and had to go in an ambulance, bad mark: I wouldn't be able to see one again. Up close, I mean. And the fish-kettle part was a bit worrying, because our mother had been bathing my arm with scalding hot bandages and pads, and that was quite bad enough, thank you. But in a fish-kettle! Three times a day.

Sometimes ... well, often, with the bandages, I had to bite a pencil to stop shouting out, and after I had chewed up two our mother just cut off the spoon part of a wooden spoon and told me to bite the handle bit. That was better because it was harder wood. Once I noticed that her eyes were a bit swimmy, but she said it was the steam from the pudding bowl of hot water. So.

Then Dr Henderson came back and I heard her say, 'Sorry. She's got it. Scarlet fever ... and he's sure to catch it now. But I'll call the ambulance and the people at Isolation. I'm sorry. I'll get on to the fumigation people as well.'

So, now I heard the worst, I opened my eyes and asked if my sister would die. And Dr Henderson looked shocked, and said, over my dead body, boy, she'll be well taken care of. And then she said to look after my mother and do everything I was told to do, because my mother was being headstrong and absolutely mad. So I had to help her. I said I would, and then she put her arm round our mother and they went down the corridor to the telephone and to see my sister.

I prayed, very hard, across the room from my bed, to my altar, not to let her die, and thought it was a jolly bad mark not to see an ambulance close to once *again*. But perhaps I'd get the scarlet fever. And that would be very interesting.

But I didn't.

Chapter 9

Sometimes, when our father had his holiday in the summer, they didn't go to France for all the time, but spent half of it with us at the cottage. That was pretty good because we often went down to the sea. Our favourite places to go were: *one*, Birling Gap, *two*, Cuckmere Haven and *three*, Newhaven. Bishopstone was pretty interesting, too, because it had some ruined cottages and a big chunk of a windmill. No one much came there because they had to cross a railway line to get to it, and that put trippers off, thank goodness, and the beach was all pebbles.

It was all pebbles at Cuckmere, and all pebbles at Birling Gap, only, there was a bit of a wrecked submarine stuck in the shingle which was very interesting. Our father said it was a German one which had got hit in the war. It was rusty, with holes and barnacles and things. At low tide you could poke about in it for sea anemones and crabs, although our father said it was rotten there for swimming.

Newhaven was pretty good because there was just one big sandy bay below the Ship Inn, under the fort, by the long jetty. When it was low tide it was really good, and not many people went there, but we did. On the other side of the huge jetty it was all pebbles and long wooden breakwaters. Once, years ago, I couldn't swim and Lally said that was rubbish, anyone could swim it was 'instinctive', like with dogs. So she gave me a bit of a shove and I fell off the breakwater and into the sea. But it wasn't

Birling Gap.

'instinctive', or whatever she called it, at all. I went down for miles, and it was all grey and swirly, and I remember seeing a huge bit of wavery seaweed floating past and I really got the wind up. Then a man in red bathing-drawers dragged me out and gave me a terrible telling off for getting *other* people into trouble! I ask you! Honestly! I had just been pushed in! But I was coughing and gasping, so I couldn't tell him. Lally was banging me on the back and thumping me on the chest and I was just hoicking up buckets and buckets of sea water which was foul-tasting, and my eyes were all running and stinging, and I thought swimming was a potty thing to do. If dogs did it easily, well, they were jolly lucky. I couldn't. And didn't.

I mean, I didn't mind shrimping. That was really jolly good. Our father came usually as well, because he liked pottering about in the rocks at Cuckmere. Sometimes *he* went swimming in his grey woollen swimming-drawers with a modesty panel. Which was a bit silly because we knew what he looked like, shaving, with no clothes on, but he didn't like undressing on the beach with strange people. Shrimping was all right because he could just roll up his flannel trousers, and we would get really masses of shrimps, all jumping and twitching, and then cover them with green seaweed to keep them fresh on the journey home.

Sometimes he would make one of his little fires in the pebbles with driftwood and we would boil the shrimps there and then, all fresh from the sea, and eat them with bread and butter. That was really the best part. Even my sister didn't mind it because Lally said that fish were cold-blooded and couldn't feel anything horrible. Mr Jane had told her that. He used to go fishing up at Teddington Lock and Eel Pie Island, and he said they never felt a *thing*. So if he said so (and he caught thousands of fish), it must be right. Anyway, it made it easier to enjoy beach-boiled shrimps.

Our mother didn't much like the seaside part. She always had a huge Japanese paper parasol, never took off her dress, and just sat in the shade reading her novels. Honestly, she might just as well have stayed at home. And she thought so too, but she quite enjoyed the tray of tea our father and Lally carried down the cliff-ladder from the café at Birling Gap. It was just a wooden shack-place, and smelled of varnish and the same blue stuff which the lady doctor used for my burned arm. There was a huge hissing tea urn on the counter, shiny buns under a glass dome and, sometimes, if you were early, sandwiches, only my father said that they tasted of good-quality linoleum, so not to bother. But you could get Fry's chocolate bars, Lally's very favourite, and coffee fudge, which our mother liked, or buy postcards of the Seven Sisters (those were the white cliffs above) and the Birling Gap Hotel. But the tea, in little metal pots, was best, with a sixpenny deposit for the tray; in case you didn't take it back. Really, that was the best part about Birling Gap. Getting down the cliff-ladder was a bit difficult, and Lally and our mother shrieked terribly when the wind blew their skirts up, but that was all part of the seaside.

It made it feel very like a holiday. If you went to Cuckmere you had to put your car in the big barn at Exceat Farm, then cross the road, through the five-barred gate, and walk all along the windey river to the beach. It was a bit of a fag, really, because we had to carry all the picnic things, the hamper, kettle, spirit stove, plus all our mother's cushions for sitting on the beach, and the shrimping-nets and bathing-towels. It was like an Arabian caravan, our father said, and it felt like it. Walking all along the riverbank . . .

There wasn't time for me to really peer into the water and see all the amazing things in the shallow streams trickling off the Cuckmere. There were little green crabs and efts and tiny flounders which skipped about in the mud, and sometimes a huge heron splashed and plashed about in the reeds, but every time I stopped to watch they all screamed out not to dawdle. So I had to hurry up, quick sharp. A bit boring really.

Except one day when we were down on the rocks, just my father and me. He was poking about in one pool, and I had the net and bucket, when he said, 'I want you to come to Newhaven tomorrow, just you, no room for anyone else. We'll go to meet the *Pevensey Castle* from Dieppe. Now, there *may* be some people we have to bring back to the cottage for a little stay. Not long. They might have luggage, so that's why I can only take you to help with things. All right?'

So I said all right, and were they friends of his and he said yes, they were very nice. He'd got a message on the telephone from *The Times*. It was all a bit of a surprise, but our mother and Lally had made the arrangements for beds and so on. So I said that was quite interesting and he said he didn't know exactly how many there would be, perhaps four, but they didn't speak any English . . . well, not much . . . but we'd have to manage for a few days, I said what do they speak, and he said, 'German. Your mother and I stayed with them in Cologne that year, remember?' Then he said that if we had enough shrimps we should get back to the others, so we walked up the beach, and he said that our mother would have told my sister, so everyone would know what was happening. Except he didn't say names or anything, just some friends.

Well, it was a funny sort of day. Lally was setting out the cups and things. Our mother was unwrapping sandwiches and singing to herself. My sister was looking at me with her I-Know-A-Secret face, a sort of smile, so I nodded at her so she would know that I knew about the people who were coming, and our father suddenly called out, 'Kettle!', which was boiling away on the stove, and I thought it was all pretty curious and secret-sounding.

At the docks at Newhaven next day we waited with a big crowd of people for the *Pevensey Castle* to get tied up. Gulls were wheeling and screaming all round the end part where the propellers were churning the water, ropes swung out across to the rails, and there was a drifting of steam from the huge orange funnel, and it was all rusty, close to, and the people standing on the decks (and there were a lot of them really) didn't do anything. I mean they didn't wave, or cheer or call to the people on the dockside. There were quite a few policemen about too. It all felt a bit peculiar. Then the gangplank rumbled up across the cobbles, and men in uniform went striding up. My father suddenly put his hand on my shoulder and said, 'There's Sutton! I can see Sutton, but not anyone else.' Then he waved, and someone by the rail waved back. I just recognized a face I knew from *The Times*. Sometimes he had come down when they were doing special photographs for the back page. So I waved too. After all, it was welcoming, and I did know him. Well, I had met him. But he didn't see me, just our father, and he raised his hand with two fingers, and my father said, aloud, 'Just two. Oh! Damn!' So I could feel he was pretty upset.

Then people started getting off and coming slowly down the gangplank, and Mr Sutton suddenly pulled two children close beside him. He bent down and spoke to them, then he pointed down to us and they half waved. When they had all got down on to the cobbles, they had to go into a big Customs place with all the other people, which my father said was for passports and papers and so on, and we'd have to wait. So we did. It was quite a funny feeling really because, although some people looked quite happy and cheerful, and met friends, there wasn't any shoving and laughing like there usually is if you come ashore. Some people were actually crying. In public. I mean, it really was pretty peculiar, and I wondered if anyone had died on the ship, or perhaps there had been an accident? But our father said no, no accident, and no one had died on the ship, as far as he knew anyway, but that these were people who had all come from Germany. When I asked why, he said it was the new rules. They were not wanted, and if they didn't leave they'd be sent to prison. I could see that he was quite upset or something because he was biting the side of his cheek, and that was always a bad sign, when we noticed him doing it.

But then he said well, there would be plenty of room in the car now, depending on how much luggage there was. I wasn't sure what it was all about, but I didn't want to ask too many questions. Not then anyway.

We went into the Customs place, where there were masses of people milling about. It was very gloomy, with yellow walls and hanging lamps with green tin shades, and there were posters on the wall of castles, like Arundel and Herstmonceux, and of lots of laughing people on beaches, and of the Southern Railway everywhere.

But no one was laughing in the crowd. They were just talking and holding bags and papers. Then Mr Sutton was there, and quite close to. Of course, I remembered him, and he shook hands, and said to my father, 'No Krauses, they didn't make it, but I've got the children.' He was looking pretty tired. His eyes were red and he hadn't even shaved. Behind him were the two children. He got them to come forward through the crowd and said, 'This is Eric, remember? His sister is Sophie. He speaks English, she doesn't. There is no luggage, just what they have.' We all shook hands, and Sophie curtsied to my father, which was a surprise, and Eric nodded his head with a short sort of jerk, and shook hands. Then we all walked into the open. Which was better. Outside, I mean.

I was going to help the girl, Sophie, with her bag, but she pulled away from me, which was a bit rude. But Mr Sutton said just let her hang on to things, they had had a dreadful time over the last few days. Our father explained about the O.M. and that Mrs Bogaerde (he didn't call her anything else to Mr Sutton) and our nanny were waiting at the cottage, and did he want to come back with us because there was plenty of room in the car and a bed at the cottage if he wanted it? But he said no, he'd just like to have a quick word, and then get up to London, and they went away together.

So we went to the O.M. and I said to Eric that they could sit in the back and I would be in front with my father, and he said, 'That is most kind of you. What is your name?' I told him, and he said he was Eric and that this, and he put his hand on her head, was his sister Sophie. He was my age, she was almost the same as my sister, so I told him that, and he looked polite and asked if they were to come in the motor car with us? I said yes. We'd go to our house and they would have a jolly nice room and had they had any food on the boat? Eric said they were too tired to eat but Mr Sutton had given them a sandwich and some tea. Which wasn't very nice to taste, and he laughed, a very little bit, when he said it, but Sophie just stood there, holding her bag, with a label fluttering on it. It said her name, *Sophie Anna Krause*. And she was crying. Without making a noise.

At the cottage our mother came running down the path through the sweet-pea trellis and the vegetables, waving like anything. I saw Lally come out to the lean-to door with a cloth in her hand, and Sophie, who was walking with me, suddenly dropped her bag and ran towards our mother and threw her arms round her knees. Our mother said, 'Sophie! Oh! Sophie! *Comment allez-vous, ma belle?*'

And I said to my father that was French and not German, and he said, 'Well, you know your mother: all foreign languages are the same to her.'

But Sophie was crying, and holding on pretty tight. Then Eric quickly came past me, picked up Sophie's bag with his own and stood before our mother. 'Good day, Aunt Maggie. I am very happy to see you!'

Our mother got up and gave him a terrific kiss, and said to come up to the house, but she looked back and raised her eyebrows at our father who just shook his head. She put a hand to her mouth, but turned away and called to Lally to come and meet the children, only, her voice was too loud, and a bit wobbly, as if she had been crying as well. But she hadn't.

My father and I walked up the path, watching Lally being introduced. Then my sister came out and everyone was in a sort of huddle shaking hands, but Sophie wouldn't leave my mother, she just hung on to her.

'Do you know them very well? Eric called our mother "Aunt *Maggie*".'

'Pretty well. She is very good with children, you know that. She'll be *very* unhappy because Mr and Mrs Krause aren't here.'

'Can I ask why, Papa?' I felt I ought to know, so as to tell my sister. Stopping down by the rhubarb clump, he said that the authorities came for Mr Krause, and Mrs Krause refused to leave him, so Mr Sutton had to take the two children during the night and got them to France, and that was all I needed to know. It was because they were Jews. All the Jews had to leave Germany now. We walked on up the path and that was that. I mean he didn't say any more, and I knew he would not. Yet.

Eric said he liked his tea very much. Lally had made them some poached eggs on toast, and even Sophie ate them, while my sister talked and talked to her and showed her all sorts of interesting things, like her cigarette card collection of film stars and a dried sea-horse and her jewel box. Well, it was only some soppy old rings from crackers and a glass bead bracelet from the lucky dip down at the vicar's sister's shop, by the Flats.

But she was being jolly kind and Sophie was *very* pretty, with huge brown eyes. She did look a bit like a big doll, which is probably what my sister liked about it all – she hardly spoke to poor Eric. Then she actually gave Sophie the bracelet, and put it on her wrist, and Lally said, 'Oh! My word! How lovely, and doesn't it suit you?' Which was pretty potty because Sophie didn't know what she was saying anyway, and it was just anyone's old bracelet really. But, I suppose, it was very nice and welcoming.

After tea Eric and I went for a walk up to the little church, and I told him about it and the cottage, and he nodded his head and smiled and seemed very interested. Then I said did he know how long they could stay? Because we could go to the Fair at the Tye down by the river next week, and he said he didn't know anything except they had some friends in somewhere called Cricklewood, and then maybe they would go to America. I thought that sounded pretty exciting, but he didn't really seem to think so. Just smiled and looked miserable behind it. So to try and cheer him up a bit I told him about how terrible it was last year for us all, and about Lally and my sister in the isolation hospital and me getting burned. I showed him my arm, which was still a bit shiny, and prickly from time to time. He was quite curious because, he said, he was going to be a doctor one day, and he hoped I was 'very recovered'. I said I was, and we just wandered back to the cottage. He wasn't interested in the Dearly Beloveds and Departed This Lifes much, didn't even look at them really, so I didn't dawdle about.

About two days later a huge car arrived in Waterloo Square in the village and some very expensive-looking people collected them, with lots of kisses and hugs, and drove them away, I suppose to the Cricklewood place. My sister said that Sophie could keep her bracelet, and we all waved and they just went. That was the last we ever saw of them. The expensive people spoke marvellous English, a *bit* Cockney, but English anyway. They kissed my mother, and the woman was wiping her eyes, and my father said it was a most dreadful world and it wasn't the sort of place he'd been fighting for in his war. The man, who was called Mr Krause also, agreed and hoped *we'd* be spared what his brother and sister-in-law had suffered. So Eric and Sophie had a *real* aunt and uncle, and that didn't make it seem quite so awful. I mean, they had kith and kin.

As long as you weren't Jewish, anyway. But they were a bit depressing. Honestly.

Mr Wilde said it was the hottest August he had ever known and it brought all the wapsies out something terrible. He wrapped up the bacon, the butter and the half of Red Leicester, and then Miss Maltravers called us from her little cage and said, 'Look what you've got! A postcard from your parents from Deauville, France. Aren't they the regular gad-abouts? And there's a letter here for Miss Jane. Postmark Richmond, so I reckon that's news from home.' But I just said thank you politely, even though I was a bit fed up because she had read our card before we had. But that was the trouble with postcards and Miss Maltravers. There was nothing you could do about it.

We went across to Wood's the butcher's with Lally's note about the mince, and the kind of blade he had to use, coarse or fine. Mr Wood, who was very fat and jolly, with his straw hat on and striped apron, said Miss Jane knew her mind all right, just what she wanted. Mrs Wood in the cash desk was fanning herself and saying upon her word, it had never been so hot, and what with the flies life was dreadful, even with all the windows open – but no draught – she felt like one of the dead chickens hanging on the rail. She looked a bit more like something else up there, but of course I didn't say so.

Outside, in the white sun, there was no one at all in the village, except two old men sitting under the chestnut tree in the shade, but stuck on the trunk of the tree there was a poster, all red and yellow: *Tilling's Zoo and Circus!* In a square under a picture of a roaring tiger there was a crayoned message saying it would be on the Tye on the 18th–19th, which was good news because that was the day after next. The Fair was already being got ready on the Tye by the church. *Brownrigg's Pleasure Rides for Families* was being set up, the middle part was already done, and the stalls were being marked out. At the end of the green they were setting up the poles for the circus tent. It was very exciting, especially because I had some money from our father put aside for the event, as Lally said, and not to be touched until then.

We'd seen all the activity on our way down from the cottage, and so after we got the 'messages' we went back to the Tye to read our postcard. Sitting in the shade I read it aloud to my sister, who was busy picking a bunch of flowers for Lally. It said, 'Darlings: Wonderful and very

The Church from the Tye.

hot, marvellous food. Do you remember this place marked X? Love, Mama.'

And I remembered all right. It was a very nice restaurant right on the promenade, and it had a big terrace where you could have drinks and ice creams, and there were waiters with white aprons, and an orchestra playing all the time, and masses of people laughing and talking and smoking. Our mother was looking really marvellous in a green turban, and she was smoking through a long green cigarette-holder, and we were with all the Chesterfields, our very best friends. There was Uncle John, and our father, and Beth, Angelica and Paul, plus our Lally and their sort-of-Lally, Miss O'Shea. We sat at a separate table, and the grown-ups were all together drinking.

There was a bit of a wind that day, and all the parasols were frilling in the wind. There were gulls high above, planing and sailing, just as they did at Newhaven and Cuckmere. The only sad thing was there was no Aunt Freda. She had eaten a bad mussel at dinner the night before, so she was what my father called 'prostrate'. It was bad luck, because I liked her best of all my pretend-aunts.

And suddenly, just as I was thinking of going to ask to be excused, I looked down at the floor and right under my foot, well almost, sort of stuck against it by the wind, was money! Paper money, quite big too. My father said it was more money than I had ever handled in my life, and then he looked around to see who it belonged to, which was a bit boring because there were simply masses of people and our mother said, 'Oh, Ulric! Finders keepers. It could be from anywhere!' So he agreed, but on condition that I shared it with the others! I mean to say, honestly.

What bad luck. That meant that I would have to share with *all* the others, three Chesterfields and my sister. So bang went my idea of the tin clockwork liner I'd seen in a shop near our hotel. It was red and white, with ten lifeboats, a black funnel where the key was and a rudder that you could actually work. But with four people to share, it would have to be sweets. So we went to a very nice sweetshop, and my father came too, to see 'fair play', he said, and to explain the money part. How much it meant in English money, and how much I had left after I'd bought Angelica a box of crystallized fruit, Beth a sort of doll who had a box of sugar almonds under her skirt, and a packet of lollipops for Paul, who only wanted yellow ones. There was quite a bit left actually, but not nearly enough for the liner. Worse luck.

I could even remember its name painted on the side – it was called '*Europa*' – in gold letters. Anyway, my father suddenly said that I had exactly enough to buy something for myself and something for poor Aunt Freda lying prostrate in her room at the hotel. It would be a very kind and thoughtful gesture (or something), he said. So I chose a box of liqueur chocolates, which I knew she liked, with lots of little chocolate bottles with coloured labels on them. I got that and then there was just enough left for me to buy a jar of mixed coloured jellies, all in the shape of fish, which I liked. But that was all. I thought it was a bit unfair. All I got out of it were the jellies, and I was sure that Angelica's fruits cost more, and so did Aunt Freda's liqueur chocolate bottles.

But when I took them up to her in her room, she was not terribly excited, she just lay on her bed with a towel on her head covering her eyes, and when I told her what I'd brought her she groaned, and made a terrible noise like choking and told me to go and find Miss O'Shea quickly. So I did. And that was all the thanks you got for being generous and making a 'thoughtful gesture'. I mean, it's potty sometimes.

So I remembered all that, sitting in the shade of the trees and watching them set up the stalls, and singing and hammering. Then my sister came back with a bunch of poppies and daisies for Lally which would all be dead before we got up the gully to the cottage in the heat. But I didn't bother to tell her. Remembering Deauville had been so miserable.

Anyway, we set off across the white bridge over the Cuckmere, along the path to the second little bridge where I fished for roach, across the road up the hill and into the gully. For shade. The funny thing was that when we climbed the rickety fence into the garden I saw Lally's apron and the basket she used for vegetables, lying all anyhow by the path, and there was a smallish vegetable marrow lying on the path itself. But no Lally.

She was sitting at the table in the kitchen, with a glass of water, and her hair all taggly (it was quite long now that she had let it grow back again), and she just gave a terrible cry and said, 'Oh Lord! Are you both all right? Where is your sister, are you safe?' And I said yes, and my sister said what's the matter? And Lally shook her head and closed her eyes. You could see she was in a state. But she drank some water, wiped her forehead and told my sister to go up to her room, quick sharp, please, and get her smelling-salts. 'They are on my dressing-table, beside my *Film Pictorials*, and hurry. I need a good sniff.'

'What happened? Was it something terrible?'

'A turn. I'm having a terrible turn. The good Lord only knows what's loose out there. And here's me having fifty fits, worrying about you coming up from the village. I should never have let you go alone, but how was *I* to know, pray, how was I to know . . .?'

My sister came down with the salts and Lally had a terrific sniff, and choked and coughed. I put the mince, the cheese and the butter in the meat-safe, and Lally said, with a hoarse voice, 'I can't believe it, never in my life. And you so *exposed*. They could have got you in a flash! How did you come up the field?' So I told her, and she wiped her eyes and put the stopper back on the bottle. 'This gets to you like a dart. So did the shock. Got to me instantly. I just ran. I don't apologize, I just ran. Without a backward look for you and your sister. Oh, the *shame* of it!'

'But what was it? What happened?'

'You didn't see them? Then they're still there . . . they are still there, *lurking*.'

'What are?'

'I don't know *what* they are! Do you think I'd have had a turn this bad if I knew what they were?'

'Well, the heifers give you a bad turn, don't they? Just potty old heifers?'

Lally got up slowly, tidying her hair, brushing down her floral. 'These weren't no heifers, my boy, you can be certain of that! These came up to me when I was getting the marrow for supper. All of a sudden. No warning. Not so much as a by-your-leave or "Here I am." Just secret, silence, until I heard this dreadful snorting and thudding, and when I turned round, over the top of the fence, just looking at me, with terrible teeth, all dripping with saliva, – stamping on the ground!' She sat down again quickly, holding her smelling-salts. 'I shall have another one. The blood has left my head. Oh! Thank the dear Lord you are safe. Your mother would have never been able to forgive me.'

'But what *were* they?'

'I tell you! How do I know what they *are*! Not *were*! If I knew, do you think I'd be taken this bad? Huge beasts, they are. Huge. Unnatural!'

My sister was looking a bit nervous. 'Perhaps they were Aleford's terrible stallions. Perhaps they are loose?'

But Lally got up again, shook herself, and said, almost in her usual sort of voice, 'I know a stallion when I see one, my lady, and these weren't no stallions. And the smell! The smell of them! It would turn your stomach. Where's the mince?'

'In the meat-safe.'

'Once through?'

'What you wrote. Mr Wood did it all just as you wrote in your note.'

'Well, you go and get the marrow. It's where I dropped it, up there. Unless they have got into the garden. That fence is not safe, not against beasts like those. We are none of us safe. I'll have to speak to your father. Leaving me all alone up on the Downs with savage things everywhere and me responsible for his children. Too much to expect of any mortal . . . too much . . .'

'There's a letter for you. Miss Maltravers gave it to us. And a card from France from our mother.'

'Why didn't you say sooner! I've been waiting and waiting for that letter.'

'You were having your turn.'

'Well, I'm better now. The salts did the trick. Where is it? And hop it, and get me my apron, the basket, the knife and the marrow. All there – I'm not going out until dusk. And mind how you go! Keep under the trees, over on the orchard side, and if you see anything, run. But leave your sister here. I can't afford to lose you both.'

My sister moaned away and said she wanted to come and see the creatures, but I had to go on my own. I wasn't really worried. I mean, if Lally had had a bad turn with the heifers it could be anything. I mean, even a St Bernard was bad enough, and an Irish wolfhound so frightened her that she locked doors. Really. Women.

It was still hot, and very quiet. I didn't see anything peculiar in the meadow. Just far away, down by the Court in the shade of the elms, there were some heifers. Or little calves. It was just when I was picking up the marrow, apron and basket, and looking about in the grass for the knife, that I realized that two of the heifers down at the Court in the shade were striped. Black and white. Of course! I remembered Tilling's Circus. There *were* two zebra down at the Court and some Shetland ponies, not heifers at all.

I went over to the rickety fence; and down by the hedge, alongside the lane, there were two huge beasts quietly cropping the long grass, shaking their heads against the flies. When I waved, one of them looked up slowly, and then they turned and came slowly ambling towards me with their enormous feet.

Here before me were the two beautiful camels which had given Lally such a turn. She was quite cross when I told them in the kitchen.

'Camels! Well, of *course* they are camels! I know a camel when I see one – the dear Lord knows how many times I've been dragged round that smelly Regent's Park. But you don't expect to see camels in the middle of the Sussex Downs, now do you? And all by yourself, looking for a marrow to feed two ungrateful children . . . It comes as a shock. You hear the sniffling, the thud, thud, you wonder what on earth, and then turn, like I did – those terrible big heads, all teeth and dribble. Give anyone a turn. Give Dracula or Frankenstein a turn.' And she started to lay the table, unfolding the tablecloth quite crossly.

'Well, your parents seem to be having a nice time. That's good. My letter was from Mrs Jane . . . she's *not* very good, a bit frail. I'll have to get along and see her soon as we get back.'

'I don't want to think about getting back.'

'Selfish boy! All you think of is yourself! Last year you had a whole four months off school with that arm, and not a stroke of work done since you went back to school. Not a stroke.'

'It's boring.'

'You'll get "boring", my boy! I reckon your father will make a few changes very soon. It's a crammer for you this September, remember that. Your last chance.' She left the table carrying the dirty plates and knives and things, clattered them into the bowl in the sink. 'Very tasty, that stuffing. Rich. A touch of Marmite always perks it up.'

She took a kettle from the Primus and poured it from a height into the bowl. I knew what was next. The drying up. And putting away. 'On your feet, if you please. Plenty of work to do across this side of the kitchen. And, Miss Fernackerpan, you take the cloth and shake it out of doors, no crumbs on my floor, and please to remember to fold it according to the creases, quick sharp, now! Camels, indeed! Whatever next, I'd like to know?'

I got the breadboard and knife and put them on the dresser. Along with her little bottle of smelling-salts. Well, I hadn't said about the two zebra down by the Court. Yet.

Chapter 10

Our father said that it was a Riley Saloon, and it had cost him a fortune. It was grey with green leather seats inside and big headlamps. I suppose it was all right really, but it wasn't anything like the O.M. It was only a square-sort-of car with wind-up windows and its name, *Riley*, written across the radiator in silver letters. The O.M. had been quite different. It was like a huge boat, all made of aluminium in Italy, with the rivets showing, and there was only one like it in all England. It had huge mudguards and headlamps, and you could fold the canvas hood right down at the back where the big strapped trunk was, where the luggage went. Now it had gone. Just like that. No warning. Just went.

One day our father arrived with this wretched Riley, and where the O.M. had always stood in the little chalk-pit down at the end of the path the new car took its place. Our father was sitting in a front seat polishing away at the wooden dashboard and just whistling as if nothing had happened. He was very pleased with the new car, but he liked all sorts of cars anyway. They were his passion. The worst thing (number one bad mark after no O.M.) was no eagle mascot on the radiator. We had *always* had the eagle there, a big silver bird with spread wings. Sitting under the tonneau at the back it was sometimes almost like flying behind him, we went so fast. But now no more. And when I asked our father where it was he just said, 'perfectly safe in the garage at Hampstead.' He hadn't sold that to the man who bought the O.M., who was a collector or something. But he didn't say anything else, just went on whistling.

And it was all because of the baby. Lally said that our mother had put her foot down and said she wasn't travelling in an open tourer with a month-old baby. And quite right too, she said. There was not enough room for us all plus a baby. A saloon was far more sensible. Anyway, *they* all thought so.

Ages and ages ago (well, a long time ago), our mother had told my sister and me that she was going to have a baby. It was a bit of a shock, I can tell you. We were up at the top end of the Hampstead garden and she was cutting lilac blossom and she suddenly just said it. Like that.

'I think you'd better know now that you are going to have a baby brother. He's in here.' And she patted her stomach where the big bump was.

Well, we had seen that she was a bit bulgy for some time, really. But Lally said she was just putting on weight. It showed quite plainly in the coat-thing she had started wearing. It was long to the ground with wide floppy sleeves and all silk with blue and gold flowers everywhere. She had said it was a Mandarin's robe, and she had bought it at the Caledonian Market for ten shillings, and wasn't that amazing? I said yes. But I didn't think it was as amazing as suddenly having a baby. Only, I didn't say. It was a bit of a surprise, I mean, but my sister had squealed and cried and jigged about. (Well, she would.) And said was it *sure* it was a little boy? And our mother said that it was kicking so hard it had to be. Or a footballer. Which I thought was a bit disgusting, really. I mean, not like rabbits or dogs or even mice. I mean, all the kicking part was a bit awful. Especially when you could actually see the bump. So. There it was. No more O.M., just a measly Riley Saloon with four doors.

But our mother had been jolly nice and decent that afternoon, and later, after supper and homework and all that, she came up to my room where I was reading and sat on the edge of my bed in her rustly Mandarin's robe and asked me if I was really pleased about the baby. So of course I said yes, remembering the awful time with the fish-kettle, and she was very pleased, you could see. She said it would be some time in July, so we wouldn't go down to the cottage right away, until she had had a bit of a rest.

Then she picked up my book and asked what I was reading, and I told her. *The Knights of the Round Table.* She said that was very suitable, and then she said, 'Oh! That's a nice name! What a good idea. That's a *terribly* nice name. Shall we call him "Gareth"?' I said all right, but if it was a girl 'Lynette' was a bit soppy. And she said yes, and gave me a kiss and went away. She was being very nice, you see, because I was eldest.

But that was all simply ages ago, and here I was sitting on the chalk bank watching our father rubbing away with the Mansion Polish singing and whistling all the time. He didn't actually speak much to me. Well, hardly noticed me really. Because he hadn't been very pleased with the report from my crammer, who had just written that I was 'a charming companion without the least shred of any application'. So that was a pretty bad mark. And a pretty rotten thing to say.

He put our father in a very bad mood, and made our mother look fearfully worried, and Lally had to go and say, 'Well, I *did* warn you!' which wasn't very cheerful, so I knew I was in the dog-house. Worse luck. It wasn't much fun, but nor was the awful 'crammer', a very boring, fat old man with a celluloid collar and buttoned boots. He sat at the end of a huge table all covered in green baize stuff and droned away at us all sitting round with our books and things. The others put up their hands to ask questions sometimes. I never did, actually. I didn't have anything to ask. And they wrote questions down in their books, and sometimes when they were standing beside him and he was explaining something in the paper they had brought to him, I would see his hand patting their bums. I mean, pretty awful really, so I just sat on mine.

From time to time a tall thin woman, with grey hair and kirby grips, would come in quietly and sit in a corner with her knitting, smiling and nodding and clicking away. And no one went up for answers then. I expect she was really a spy of some sort. I never spoke to her, but she nodded at me. I bet she wrote that foul report about me which made my father so cross.

Anyway, I wrote a play. It wasn't bad. It was so boring just sitting there and listening to terrible talks about logarithms or, worse still, something they called another sort of 'log', but this was about anagrams and word puzzles.

I mean, you do see? It was the wrong place for me. So that's why I was in trouble with our father, who suddenly got up, put the lid back on his tin of Mansion Polish and said, pretty rudely I thought, 'Are you *still* there? Just sitting?' (Well! he could perfectly well see I was.) So I said yes, but I supposed that he was a bit fed up about the crammer. And he said he wasn't actually cock-a-hoop, and neither would I be when I got up to Glasgow and the new school, because they were really strict up there, and I'd be 'grounded in a decent education' whether I liked it or not. He just wished it was a boarding-school, to bring me to my senses. But I was too old because I was thirteen, and our mother had said no. (Thank goodness.)

Then he looked at his pocket watch, and told me to remember that this was my very last chance. I had three years left to pull myself together. He was chewing the side of his cheek, which was the bad sign, but all he said after that was to go up and tell Lally that he was ready to give her a lift to the village, and I'd better go with her to carry the paraffin can. Then he slammed the door of the Riley pretty hard and said, 'Just remember that we are not expected to fail in this family.'

So I didn't say anything. I was a bit depressed, honestly.

Driving down to the village Lally sat in front with him, and they talked away about how nice the car was, and she said, 'Remember the Salmson? Wasn't that a pretty car?' But all she really meant was that it had little glass vases in the back where you could put flowers if you picked them on a picnic, and she thought it was quite marvellous to drive along in a car with glass vases with *real* water and flowers in them. I mean, it was all pretty silly. But they didn't talk to me. I remembered the Salmson very well, and how he used to drive it round and round the course at Brooklands. A bit showy-off ... but it was his passion. Anyway, he dropped us off at Waterloo Square, and drove back off to London. When I asked Lally why there had been all the rushing and packing, she said that something had happened at *The Times* and Mr Hitler was now the King of Germany or something. She didn't rightly know, but she hoped that Fred the Fish had got some whiting or, perhaps better still, some cod for a fish pie tonight. Of course, it was Friday, so Fred the Fish was by the Market Cross with his stall and the scales and his little Morris van, which was rather bashed now.

There were one or two people I knew round his stall, and he was making them laugh a bit, all except Beattie Fluke, who was there in her black tammy, which looked green really, it was so old. And she was quite worried, not smiling as she usually did with her awful no-teeth-mouth. 'I got a nice bit of rock salmon for Mr Fluke,' she said. 'Although I don't know as he's got the stummick to eat it. Can't hold anything down, not with all the worry.'

Lally said, very kindly, while Fred the Fish was cutting her a chunk of cod, 'You've got trouble? I am sorry.'

Beattie Fluke shrugged her woollen cardigan over her shoulders and said, 'Haven't you heard then? It's all over. The Alefords are selling up. Off to Canada! So now what's to become of us? Mr Fluke was the best herdsman this side of Chichester. If they sell up, bang goes his herd. Then what? What happens to the cottage then? I been in that cottage all my married. If they sell the herd he'll get the boot. Then what?'

It *was* pretty worrying. After all that stuff from our father, now this. Even Lally looked anxious when she took her packet of cod, wrapped in newspaper, from Fred, and put it in the old red and black basket. 'Now, Mrs Fluke, don't you fret yourself. I expect it's all just a rumour. You

know how rumours start in the summer, especially in the
heat. Like fish going off . . .'

Beattie Fluke said that fish going off was no rumour.
She knew that for a *fact*. It was not like the *real* rumour
she had got hold of. And then she turned to Miss Annie
from Baker's (who had got blown through the window
with the bucket of petrol ablaze) and asked her if they'd
heard any rumours in the shop? But Miss Annie just said
she was like the three monkeys: see, speak and hear no
rumours. So she didn't rightly know. Beattie Fluke just
whispered that her poor head was still addled, and it was
time for her 'cup of tea'. We watched her go across to the
Magpie and push open the public bar door, and Lally said
she'd get a lot more rumour in there.

We walked back down the path to the river. I was
carrying the paraffin can, which was pretty heavy and
kept on clonking my knee, and Lally was swinging the
shopping-bag very fast, from side to side, to frighten away
any adders. She said that adders liked to lie in the dusty
path in hot sun like today, and they would just rear up
and snap at you unless you watched out. She always did
this on very hot days, only this time I could see she was a
bit worried about Mrs Fluke's rumour. So was I. It was a
bit unsettling, especially after our father's mood, and Scotland, and the dreadful school in September.

'I tell you what,' she said. 'When you go down to
Court Farm for the milk this afternoon, keep a sharp eye
open for Len Diplock. He'll be in the yard somewhere.
Mucking about with his harness and waggons. Getting
polished up for harvest next month. Have a casual word
with him. Act as if you didn't know, just heard it at the

Market Cross, ask if it was just gossip. Sure as sure he'll say yes. Gossip!'

'But if I see Miss Aleford? What then? She's bound to be in the dairy, doing the skimming and everything.'

Lally shook her head and stopped swinging the bag, and we crossed over the little bridge up to the road. 'Depends. If she is friendly. Depends. You'd have to go carefully. If it was true, about Canada and so on, I swear she'd have told your father. Said something.'

We started up the side of the gully. Skylarks spun up out of the tussocky grass of the meadow, and fat white clouds drifted gently down towards Cuckmere Haven. It couldn't be really true. Just a Beattie Fluke rumour. I hoped. I even crossed my fingers.

My sister said she couldn't come down for the milk because the baby might cry. I said it had been crying for weeks anyway, and there were two quart cans to carry on account of we used so much milk now, and she would have to come. And Lally said, 'Shoo! Shoo! Get from under my feet, and bring me back a half-dozen eggs, I'll need some for the fish pie.'

So we walked down the hedge path with the cans and a basket, and I told my sister the bad rumour and she shook her head and said it couldn't happen. There was no Len Diplock in the yard, worse luck, and I couldn't see him in the cart shed, but I could hear Miss Aleford singing. In the dairy. That was a bit of a worry, so we pushed open the door into the cool, damp, milky-smelling place, and there she was, stretching big muslin squares over all the bowls and dishes to keep the flies off. She was looking quite all right, in a cotton dress with little puffy sleeves like a real woman, and a big straw hat on top of her earphones, and tennis socks and tennis shoes. She was singing 'T'was on the Isle Of Capri That I Met Him', but she petered out when she heard the door squeal open, and turned round quickly.

'Heigh ho! Heigh ho! Goodness me today! Gave my heart a flutter, you did. Quite carried off ... Milk? Eggs by the look of it, your basket an' all. And you know Miss Jane owes us one shilling and ninepence. I'll overlook the ha'penny,' and she put a bundle of muslin on the shelf above the slate ones covered with the milk bowls. 'It's the Fresh, now, isn't it? With the baby an' all. My word, how the time goes. A week has gone before you can catch your breath.' She started to ladle out into our cans and told my sister to choose her eggs from the big crock by the door. 'The ones with dirt and feathers on them are no fresher than the rest. They only *look* as if an old hen had just dropped one in the nettles five secs ago. Brought your money?'

I had, wrapped up in paper, and while she was closing the lids of the cans my sister said, quite suddenly without any warning, 'Is it true you are going to Canada, Miss Aleford?' and Miss Aleford got such a shock she turned her head too quickly and her straw hat went all wonky. 'Who said?' she said very crossly. 'Where did you pick up that little nugget of misinformation, I'd like to know? Those Daukeses, I'll be bound. Gossip-mongers both. Live in the Magpie. There's more lies spilled in that bar than in the House Of Commons!'

So I said, pretty quickly, that no, it wasn't the Daukeses,

but just someone down at Fred the Fish's stall in Waterloo
Square, I didn't know who. Miss Aleford pushed her hat
back on her head, licked her finger with spittle, and wiped
out '1/9½d. Rectory' on the slate on the wall.

'Well,' she said, pushing the cans across the big shelf,
'we have it in mind. Not certain. Thinking about it. My
brothers want to start over somewhere else. Not me. But
I'm not asked . . .'

'Where would you go?' said my sister. 'Miles away?'

And Miss Aleford began to sort out her bundle of
muslin. 'Vancouver. There are some cousins near there,
lots of opportunity.' So I said that was very far away, and
when would they go to Vancouver, and she was snappy
and said she was sure she didn't know, but after the harvest
and before the spring sowing. People called the Wintle-
Pughes were very interested in the land, but they didn't
want the buildings, so they'd go up for auction. And my
sister said what was that? Miss Aleford just said, 'Now be
off with you, I've got work to do. Any questions, you ask
Stapleford's in Lewes, they are the agents, not me.
Anyway,' she said when we started out of the door,
'anyway, it's rumours. Just rumours. No need to fret. Yet.'
And she started singing the Capri song again. We could
hear her until we were quite far up the lane and then the
singing faded away and all you could hear was our feet
patting slowly along in the chalky dust. We didn't say
anything to each other because we were both having a
think.

'Why do you call it Waterloo Square when it's the
Market Cross? You always do.'

'That's its real name. The soldiers who went to fight at

Waterloo were shut up in the cottages by the chestnut tree. And then they went to the ships at Newhaven. I wonder if our father knows about the auction business? Or our mother. It's very worrying.'

My sister said she didn't know what an auction was, so I told her the one who paid the most money would get the house or cottage, and that was worrying because our father kept saying he hadn't a bean.

Our mother was sitting under the apple trees in the little orchard when we got over the fence, and put her finger to her lips because the baby was asleep just behind her in its pram. But she whispered that she didn't know about the auction, but that she'd speak to our father when he came back next week.

Lally was in the kitchen lining a pudding bowl with slices of white bread for the summer pudding, and beside her there was a big bowl of gooseberries, blackcurrants and loganberries. And I knew jolly well what that meant. Topping and tailing, which was terribly boring and fiddly. And of course I was quite right. She took the milk and the eggs and told us to sit down and get to work while she started on the fish pie. It was all a bit annoying, because it was hot and sunny outside, and we had to sit topping and tailing. Anyway, you just couldn't argue.

'You want summer pudding, you have to work for it. Won't get a single thing in this life, not unless you do a bit of work. Won't enjoy it if it hasn't cost you labour.'

But I didn't say anything except about the auction and that really made her stop. It worried her, you could see that easily by the way she started to skin the chunk of cod. She was quite rough with it, and the knife was stabbing about. She pulled the skin off in strips and dumped them on a tin plate.

'Well, you got that much out of the lady. Vancouver. Fancy. Almost halfway to Japan or as near as makes no difference. So that'll be that. Give me a couple of old eggs from the lean-to, I can't boil the fresh ones for the fish pie ... and while I boil them, you might go down and pump me a couple of buckets for the washing-up.'

So I said, 'What about the gooseberries?' and she said Miss Fernackerpan could carry on with those. *She'd* need the hot water as soon as she'd got the fish on to boil. So I clonked down with the two buckets feeling a bit funny inside. The idea of the cottage going up for the auction was very frightening, especially with no money. And then I'd be up in awful school in Scotland, and perhaps I'd never know what had happened. I felt really mouldy.

In the kitchen Lally was banging about and things were boiling and she said 'Drat' once or twice, and my sister said she'd finished the fruits and she'd like to see the baby. If it was awake.

'If it's awake I reckon you'd know. It's a proper little crier. Enough tears he sheds to float that Cunarder. You might be able to see that? Biggest ship in the world? September up in Scotland. That's something to look forward to – Out of my way, this is a pan of boiling water!' My sister just went off into the orchard. Lally set the boiled eggs on a saucer to cool. 'This cottage needs a lot doing to it. A lot. No water, no taps, no electric light, no heat nor what we supply by logs, no telephone, and with a baby in the place you *have* to have those things. And that privy! I ask you! How ever is your mother going to manage if I have to leave ... which I will one day, you know? Mrs Jane is really frail and Mr Jane as deaf as a post. They will need me one of these days.'

'But you wouldn't go? Leave us? You couldn't!'

'I would, my boy, if I *had* to. That privy, no light, no water, and, bye the bye, tonight I'll thank you to take your spade up to the top and dig the hole for you-know-what!'

'Already! I did it three days ago. Something like that.'

'It's *nothing* like that. Five people in the place now! Different when we are just three. Very different ... But if my own flesh and blood need me, what do I do? You are going away, and you're grown up now, you don't need me. Your sister is getting on, too. And she's got the baby to tend. I wouldn't leave you until we had everything nicely settled here. But I do hope your father gives it a lot of thought when the auction comes up. He should get this place for sixpence with all that's wrong with it. It's a hovel, a real hovel, if you think about it. Now then, if the eggs are cool enough, peel them, in a bowl of water, can't abide bits of shell all over my sink. Clogs the drains ... And that's just *another* thing! Drains!'

But I didn't listen, she was making everything sound so terrible. It was like the end of the world.

It felt a bit better sitting round the table all together in the kitchen at dinner. The baby had been fed and was asleep in its basket, the windows were open, and the smell of the nicotiana was really strong, even though we had eaten fish pie. Our mother had a little half-bottle of white wine on the table, and it was very nice all being together, which is what made thinking about *not* being together make me feel so miserable. It came and went away like toothache. Lally and our mother were talking about all the things wrong with the place and what it was like in summer and in winter and now with the baby ... They just didn't say anything cheerful. My sister had a second helping of summer pudding and said she simply loved the baby and wasn't it awful that they had to grow up? Lally said, in a jokey voice, well, only if they grew up to be as wilful and spoiled as me. But even if she didn't mean it really, I felt it was perhaps what she actually meant. And my mother put her hand on mine, across the table, and said she loved me anyway. After all I had got the Second Chance now in Scotland, and she was sure I'd be sensible and please our father. Lally asked that *if* I had got my strength back, having eaten so much, to remember the spade was in the lean-to, and it was cool enough now. She would do the washing-up as soon as the kettles boiled. My sister said could she be excused from the Bindie Bucket this time, because she wanted to keep an eye on the baby. But Lally said that our mother and she had four perfectly good eyes, thank you very much, and ears too, and that boiling kettles was *another* thing that was wrong with the cottage. Drain, privies, boiling kettles and steeping nappies! It was getting to her quick as a dart. And our mother laughed, finished her glass of wine and started clearing the table.

So I thought I'd better go and dig the hole. I could get away from them all for a bit, but I wouldn't be able to have a real think, because you can't when you are digging a hole and the earth is dry, and there are tangly roots, and you have to be careful that the ground isn't squashy where you had dug before. (That was a terrible bad mark.)

In the lean-to I heard our mother telling Lally that things had to change really. A growing family now, and that she was pretty fed up with going down to the Star to telephone and up the garden to sit in a hut with a view of the orchard and an inquisitive hare. And they both laughed together, and I heard the clatter and chink of the plates and forks, and wandered up to the top of the garden myself. With the spade.

After I had dug the hole, not very far away from the privy on account of all the carrying, I got the big pole ready and marked the place with a branch, so we'd be able to see it in the light of the hurricane lamp when it was dark, and then I wandered back to the cottage with the spade over my shoulder.

It was no good trying to have a think at that time. I was all a bit muddled anyway, and then suddenly, flickering through the high hedge running along Great Meadow on the lane side I saw something blue. Bright blue, with bits of silver twinkling in the last of the light. You hardly ever saw a car going up our lane. Only carts, or the reaper. But this was a very fast blue car!

I ran down the path and when I got to the little chalk-pit place where the Riley had been I saw Ted Deakin coming up from the lane. He waved a piece of paper over his head. 'A message, for your mother. On the telephone. Half-hour ago. Mrs Fry at the Star wrote it down. I was in the yard and she knew I were running in my motor. You want to see it? Blue. Very smart. Austin Ten. So she said nip up the top and give them this message. So I did. You want to have a look? I'm going to give Ron Daukes a ride down to the Magpie . . . If there is any answer . . .'

I said it was very kind of him, and I'd get our mother and if there was an answer I'd come back. He'd said he'd be at the Daukeses' for ten minutes because Ron was very slow in his movements. In the kitchen Lally was drying her hands on a towel, our mother had stacked the washing-up bowls in the sink, and she took the message in its envelope and said, 'Whatever can this be? It must be from *The Times*. It's Daddy.' She started to read the note, shook her head, put her hand to her face, and said, 'Oh! Dear Lord!'

'Is there an answer for Mr Deakin?' I said. She said no, no answer, so I ran to the Daukeses' and shouted through their gate (the front door was open), and Mrs Daukes came out with a basket of greenstuff for her rabbits. When I said, 'No reply, thank you very much,' she just called over her shoulder, 'No answer, Ted,' and I ran away and she went off down the garden. Didn't even look at me. She really was a bit rude, but I didn't care.

Our mother was sitting quite still at the table, and Lally and my sister were standing by her looking anxious. She seemed a bit funny, and when I said, 'Is it about our father?' she just said yes. And then she read the note aloud.

'Arriving tomorrow about 10 a.m. Amy in Brighton with pneumonia. Stable but ill. News when I see you.' Then she laid the pieces of paper on the table.

'Do you know what it means?' I said, and Lally nearly raised her hand to give me a bit of a cuff for rudeness, but I was too far away, and our mother said that she *thought* she knew. But that Mrs Fry had got the name wrong. She had spelled it 'A-M-Y' like a girl, but it should have been 'A-I-M-E', which was a man's name. And my sister said but we don't know anyone with that name, and our mother said that we didn't at present, but we would pretty soon, because that was our grandfather's name.

'But we haven't got a grandfather in England!' I said.

Our mother said, with a tired sort of voice, 'Well, I rather think that you have now. Brighton! I ask you. After all these years. Ill with pneumonia and everyone thought he was long dead somewhere in Brazil. Poor Ulric! My poor darling . . .'

She got up slowly, with the pieces of paper scrunched up in her hand, and went out into the vegetable garden, and Lally said to let her be, it had been a bit of a shock for her, as it had for us all. Who'd have thought it? Let's just go on as before, and have you dug that hole, I would like to know? And there was a bit of wick-trimming to do before dark. She was being pretty bossy again, but it was quite good to have something to do this time.

A bit later, after we had washed the chimneys and trimmed the oily wicks with nail scissors, I was able to go out just as it was starting to get dusk and the swallows were swooping about after the midges and gnats. Then our mother came back to the cottage and she said that she'd probably have to go to Brighton tomorrow, and she didn't know how long for but we were to be helpful and not tear about because Lally had the baby to look after. And Lally said she'd deal with its feeds, and she was sure we'd behave. Usually, she said, it was as dangerous as boiling milk with us two. Turn your back for a second and it was trouble. And my sister said it was very exciting to have a real kith and kin grandfather that we never expected, and our mother just nodded, smiling in a very sad sort of way, and went upstairs to the baby.

Wick-Trimming.

In the garden the shadows were growing long, and the light was orangy-gold, but far away, right above High-And-Over, there was a long line of dark cloud, quite flat like a cover, drifting in from the sea, and the evening star was burning just on the edge, and then a little breeze came riffling through the sweet-pea canes and jostled the big leaves of the rhubarb clump, and the swallows spun and dived, making screaming and mewing sounds, and I went down to the Daukeses' hedge to the same place where I had seen Minnehaha all that time ago, and the old flower-pot was still there, cracked, in the long grass. So I sat there. To have a bit of a think.

Up at the cottage I heard a door shut. My sister laughed suddenly, and called 'Coming!', and then Lally went past a window singing her new song, '. . . a thin golden ring on her finger, dum de dum dum the Isle of Caprieeee . . .' and it got cut off then, because, I suppose, she went off upstairs. Someone shut a window quite hard, with a bang. And then everything was still.

But I just sat where I was with the shadows getting long.

Having a think.

D.v.d.B
London, 14.3.92

Discover more about our forthcoming books through Penguin's FREE newspaper...

Penguin
Quarterly

It's packed with:

- exciting features
- author interviews
- previews & reviews
- books from your favourite films & TV series
- exclusive competitions & much, much more...

Write off for your free copy today to:
Dept JC
Penguin Books Ltd
FREEPOST
West Drayton
Middlesex
UB7 0BR
NO STAMP REQUIRED

READ MORE IN PENGUIN

In every corner of the world, on every subject under the sun, Penguin represents quality and variety – the very best in publishing today.

For complete information about books available from Penguin – including Puffins, Penguin Classics and Arkana – and how to order them, write to us at the appropriate address below. Please note that for copyright reasons the selection of books varies from country to country.

In the United Kingdom: Please write to *Dept. JC, Penguin Books Ltd, FREEPOST, West Drayton, Middlesex UB7 OBR*

If you have any difficulty in obtaining a title, please send your order with the correct money, plus ten per cent for postage and packaging, to *PO Box No. 11, West Drayton, Middlesex UB7 OBR*

In the United States: Please write to *Penguin USA Inc., 375 Hudson Street, New York, NY 10014*

In Canada: Please write to *Penguin Books Canada Ltd, 10 Alcorn Avenue, Suite 300, Toronto, Ontario M4V 3B2*

In Australia: Please write to *Penguin Books Australia Ltd, 487 Maroondah Highway, Ringwood, Victoria 3134*

In New Zealand: Please write to *Penguin Books (NZ) Ltd,182–190 Wairau Road, Private Bag, Takapuna, Auckland 9*

In India: Please write to *Penguin Books India Pvt Ltd, 706 Eros Apartments, 56 Nehru Place, New Delhi 110 019*

In the Netherlands: Please write to *Penguin Books Netherlands B.V., Keizersgracht 231 NL–1016 DV Amsterdam*

In Germany: Please write to *Penguin Books Deutschland GmbH, Friedrichstrasse 10–12, W–6000 Frankfurt/Main 1*

In Spain: Please write to *Penguin Books S. A., C. San Bernardo 117–6° E–28015 Madrid*

In Italy: Please write to *Penguin Italia s.r.l., Via Felice Casati 20, I–20124 Milano*

In France: Please write to *Penguin France S. A., 17 rue Lejeune, F–31000 Toulouse*

In Japan: Please write to *Penguin Books Japan, Ishikiribashi Building, 2–5–4, Suido, Tokyo 112*

In Greece: Please write to *Penguin Hellas Ltd, Dimocritou 3, GR–106 71 Athens*

In South Africa: Please write to *Longman Penguin Southern Africa (Pty) Ltd, Private Bag X08, Bertsham 2013*

BY THE SAME AUTHOR

Four volumes of Dirk Bogarde's bestselling and highly acclaimed autobiography:

A Postillion Struck by Lightning

With superlative skill and power, Dirk Bogarde evokes his early life, from the idylls of childhood to his arrival in Hollywood. 'What emerges ... is a whole life. Whole in the sense that the sensitive, shy, brilliant human being called Dirk Bogarde speaks to you as you read — Dilys Powell in the *Sunday Times*

Snakes and Ladders

The years from the Second World War to the making of *Death in Venice* – spellbinding years in which Bogarde transformed himself from the matinée idol of the 'Doctor' films into one of the finest screen actors of our time.

An Orderly Man

As work on Visconti's *Death in Venice* draws to a close, Dirk Bogarde is preparing his house in Provence as a retreat. Before he is rewarded with the peace and tranquility he craves, however, he is forced to endure damage to his possessions, dying olive trees and the rampaging Mistral.

Backcloth

The fourth volume of Dirk Bogarde's autobiography, *Backcloth* is also the most intimate and searching. Based on personal letters, notebooks and diaries, it explores the patterns of happiness and pain that have made up his life. From the busy eccentric family home in Hampstead to a secluded farmhouse in Provence, *Backcloth* highlights the people, emotions and experiences that forged the man from the child.

BY THE SAME AUTHOR

A Particular Friendship

They were strangers and opposites and never met, and yet they enjoyed a passionate and unusual friendship. In 1967, Dirk Bogarde, then at the height of his fame, received a letter from America from a complete stranger who had once lived in his house. Intrigued, he wrote back to her and thus began a flood of correspondence that ended with her death in 1972.

'Only gradually does it emerge how much this correspondence meant to Dirk Bogarde himself . . . An absorbing volume in the mould of *84 Charing Cross Road*' — *Spectator*

A Gentle Occupation

1945. The last outpost of a fading Empire. And the final savagery of a forgotten war . . . Hostilities have ceased with the ending of the war in South-East Asia. But on one island in the Java Sea, 400 miles south of Singapore, the fragile truce is plunged into the chaos of violence and nationalist uprising. As an Empire crumbles, it is those who remain to keep the peace who must fight the hardest to survive . . . 'An irresistible writer – *Sunday Times*. 'Wonderful . . . Dirk Bogarde shines in his dialogue and characterization' – *New Statesman*

BY THE SAME AUTHOR

Voices in the Garden

On the private beach of her palatial villa in the South of France, Cuckoo Peverill, a faded beauty, has filled her pockets with stones and walked into the sea. Marcus Pollock, a young handsome man from England, saves her from her fate and he and his girlfriend Leni are invited to spend their vacation in the opulent Peverill home. 'A sense of beauty immediately engages the reader's attention and brings the book alive' – *Spectator*

Jericho

Writer William Caldicott's life is complicated enough. He is about to embark on divorce proceedings when he receives a cryptic letter of farewell from his estranged brother James together with the key to his house in a remote French village.

West of Sunset

'It wasn't an accident, you know. With Hugo. It was deliberate. He drove into that truck quite deliberately in his white Maserati . . .' Set amid the gaudy wastes of Los Angeles, *West of Sunset* is a savage, funny and romantic story from a novelist at the height of his powers. 'Very engaging' – *Observer*